DISCOVERING HISTORY

75

THE MAKING OF THE
United Kingdom

PETER HEPPLEWHITE and NEIL TONGE

Series Editors
NEIL TONGE &
PETER HEPPLEWHITE

Causeway Press Ltd

To Marie and Marion

Acknowledgement

Our thanks to Mike Haralambos.

Peter Hepplewhite
Neil Tonge
May, 1992

Note to teachers

1. **The Focus pages**
    Each chapter contains a Focus page which aims to engage the reader, excite curiosity and raise issues. All Focus pages are based on primary source material.

2. **The Sources**
    Most of the written sources are taken from original documents. In some cases the language has been adapted to aid comprehension.

    All original artwork is based on primary source material - either literary, pictorial or archaeological.

3. **The Teachers' Guide**
    A teachers' guide is available. It is photocopiable and provides assessment tests, guidance for marking, advice for teaching, additional information and worksheets with further activities including games and simulations.

CONTENTS

1 INTRODUCTION

DATA FILE: *The British Isles, 1500-1550*

SCOTLAND
Capital Edinburgh. A poor climate for agriculture with little good farming land. Main exports linen, coal and salt. The country is divided between the English speaking lowland Scots and the Gaelic speaking highlanders. Dislike of the English is one of the few things that unites the Scots. The Stuart family holds the throne.

ENGLAND
Capital London. A rich, fertile land. Main exports wool and woollen cloth. Small iron, coal and salt industries. Ruled by the Tudor family. England seeks to control the other countries of the British Isles to stop enemies in Europe, such as France, using them as allies.

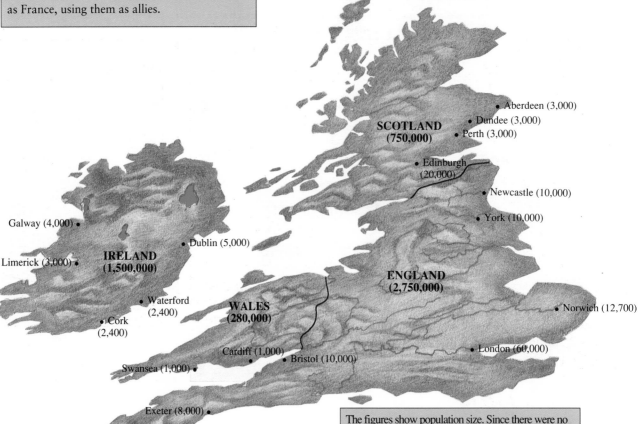

SCOTLAND (750,000)

Aberdeen (3,000)
Dundee (3,000)
Perth (3,000)
Edinburgh (20,000)
Newcastle (10,000)
York (10,000)

Galway (4,000)

IRELAND (1,500,000)

Dublin (5,000)

Limerick (3,000)

ENGLAND (2,750,000)

Waterford (2,400)

WALES (280,000)

Norwich (12,700)

Cork (2,400)

Cardiff (1,000)

London (60,000)

Swansea (1,000)

Bristol (10,000)

Exeter (8,000)

The figures show population size. Since there were no censuses (counting of people) the figures are estimates.

IRELAND
The Irish people are mostly poor farmers, deeply loyal to their clan chieftains. The main language in the countryside is Gaelic. The Irish chieftains are frequently at war with each other. The English Tudor monarchs control the area around Dublin. They call themselves 'Lords of Ireland' and want to conquer the rest of the country.

WALES
Capital Cardiff. A country of poor soil and scattered farms. Wales had been conquered by Edward I in the 13th century and was officially united with England in 1536. However, the Welsh remain a proud and distinct people.

Tudors and Stuarts

To help them study, historians break the past into periods of time, each with its own title. The 250 years covered by this book, from 1500-1750, almost matches the Tudor and Stuart period.

This title comes from the surname of the royal families. The first Tudor monarch, Henry VII, began his reign in 1485. The last Stuart monarch, Queen Anne, died in 1714.

A second title for these years is the Early Modern Age. This title fits well. During this time the country as we know it today began to take shape. The people thrashed out answers to key political and religious questions. These included:

What kind of Christians would the British be, Catholics or Protestants?

How should Britain be governed? How much power should monarch and Parliament have?

How far would the powerful country of England dominate her weaker neighbours – Scotland, Wales and Ireland? Should they join together to form a United Kingdom?

Each question led to bloody war or rebellion. It was a dangerous time in British history, a time that made the nation we know today.

Source A   King Henry VII

The Tudor King Henry VII took the crown by force. He defeated Richard III at the battle of Bosworth in 1485.

Source B   Queen Anne

The Stuart Queen Anne died in 1714. She had outlived all her children and Parliament invited her cousin, the German George of Hanover, to become king.

Source C

PASSPORT

Activities

1. Look at the data file. Which country was the most powerful? Give reasons for your answer.

2. What other periods of history have you studied? What were they called and why were they given this title?

3. How did the Tudor family come to rule Britain? Why did the Stuart family stop ruling Britain? In what ways do your answers show a problem in being ruled by kings and queens?

4. If you were asked your nationality what answer would you give? Look at Source C. What does it indicate about the future of the United Kingdom?

2 RELIGIOUS CONFLICT

The timeline (tree)

1642-1649
Civil war breaks out in England. Many of the king's followers are members of the Church of England. The followers of Parliament are mainly Puritans.

1620
Some strict Protestants called Puritans think the Church of England is too Catholic. Some leave on the *Mayflower* ship for America.

1611
James I prints the official Bible which all people in the Church of England must use in worship.

1558-1603
Elizabeth makes the Church of England Protestant. Her Parliament passes laws against Catholics.

1560
In Scotland John Knox sets up the Church of Scotland. They are much stricter Protestants than the Church of England.

1534
Henry VIII quarrels with the Pope. He makes himself Head of the Church of England.

1517
Martin Luther, a German monk, writes a long attack upon the Catholic Church. Many of his followers break with the Catholic Church.

1325 - 1384
John Wycliffe criticises the Pope as too rich and too powerful. He translates the Bible from Latin into English. This was forbidden by the Pope.

Catholic Church

Christian Church 1 AD

Themes

In 1500 most people in Britain were Catholics. They saw the Pope as leader of the Church. By 1750 most people were Protestants. They did not accept the leadership of the Pope.

This split of the Christian Church into Catholics and Protestants is known as the Reformation. The word comes from reform, which means to change for the better. Protestants struggled against what they saw as wrong with the Catholic Church. Protestant comes from the word protest. What happened in Britain was part of a bitter clash that took place in many European countries.

This chapter looks at the following questions.

- Why did many people turn against the Catholic Church?
- Who were the Protestants and what did they believe in?
- Why did King Henry VIII quarrel with the Pope and set up the Church of England?
- Why did Protestants argue with each other after they had left the Catholic Church?

We begin with the death of a Catholic martyr. A martyr is a person who is put to death for refusing to give up their beliefs. Queen Elizabeth I ordered that all Christians worship as Protestants. In the Focus, Margaret Clitheroe refuses to give up her Catholic faith.

Focus Activities

1. Choose three words which you think best describe Margaret's actions. Give reasons for the words you have chosen.

2. Why was Margaret given such a cruel death?

3. A history book written for Catholic children in 1971 said that Margaret's husband, John Clitheroe, 'was really broken-hearted, and yet he did not use his suffering to turn to God. He could not really have loved Margaret'. Is this a fair thing to say about John Clitheroe?

Margaret Clitheroe, a Catholic martyr

Margaret Clitheroe walked across the narrow Ouseburn Bridge at York on the morning of March 25, 1586. Her few steps took her from prison to her place of execution in the Tollbooth.

It was Good Friday and the bridge was crowded. News of Margaret's coming death had shocked the city. Yet she walked calmly, even happily amongst the people, passing out alms (money) to the poor. Now there was no going back.

Margaret was a Catholic and a recusant. This meant she refused to give up the old faith. She would not go to church and use the new Protestant prayer books. She had sheltered Catholic priests in her home. For this she was called a traitor.

For over ten years Margaret had led a dangerous life. She had seen the grisly remains of executed Catholics displayed on Micklegate Bar, one of York's main gates. She knew the risks she ran.

John Clitheroe, her husband, was a wealthy butcher. He was an important and popular man who had served as one of the city's treasurers. He was content to worship as the government told him. John was troubled and worried about his wife but could not persuade Margaret to give up her faith.

On Monday, March 10th, Margaret was arrested. A young servant, threatened with a beating, betrayed his mistress. He had shown the secret hiding place for priests.

Brought before Judge Clinch, Margaret refused to stand trial. She realised the main witnesses would have been her children. They would have been threatened, beaten and forced to condemn their own mother.

For doing this Margaret faced a grim punishment. The sentence for refusing to stand trial was death by crushing. She was badly frightened and came close to breaking on Tuesday, March 22nd, when the sheriffs came and told her she was to die on the coming Friday.

Margaret collapsed and pleaded with a friend to take a message out to other Catholics to pray for her. For the last three days of her life she refused to eat. During this time she came to terms with her fate and her God.

On that last morning her courage was too much for the city officials who had little stomach for their work. The Sergeants who should have killed her hired four beggars, men desperate enough to do anything, to take their place. In the Tollbooth Margaret was stripped and tied down, face upwards on the ground. A sharp stone, about the size of a man's fist, was pushed under her back. Her face was covered with a handkerchief and then the heavy door laid on her. Quickly, clumsily, the beggars began to heave large stone weights on top.

As the pressure increased Margaret groaned a last prayer, 'Jesu! Jesu! Jesu! Have mercy upon me'. Then there was silence except for the sound of her body being crushed.

The Catholic Church

By 1500 the Catholic Church was already very old. Its leader was the Pope who was believed to be God's spokesman on earth. From the Vatican Palace in Rome he controlled cardinals, bishops, priests, monks and nuns across Western Europe. They passed on his words to the people.

However not everyone was content with the Catholic Church. Some believed that it had moved away from true Christianity. Its leaders were failing in their duties. They had become too rich, powerful and corrupt. Some people wanted to worship in different ways. They were called heretics and could be punished by death.

Source A   The Pope

The Pope was in many ways like a king. He ruled over his own country in Italy. To some people Popes seemed more interested in politics and wars than looking after the Church. This painting shows the court of Pope Pius II.

Source B   The Mass

The Mass was the most important Catholic service. Bread and wine were blessed by the priest and said to become the body and blood of Christ. During the Mass only the priest was allowed to go near the altar. He was the link between God and the people.

Source C   The Latin Bible

The Bible was written in Latin. This was the language of the Romans. It linked the Church to the days when Jesus was alive and was used by the priests for services. Only a few people could understand it. Bibles in English were illegal. Many churchmen were against translating the Bible as this might encourage people to form their own opinions about God.

Source D   Relics

These were objects believed to be especially holy. Priests might claim them to be pieces of the Cross or the bones of saints. Often they were believed to have special powers, for example healing the sick.

Source E   Images

Statues and pictures, especially of Mary, the mother of Jesus, were thought to be important in helping people pray. They reminded those who couldn't read about the story of Jesus. Some statues were thought to contain the spirits of saints who could work miracles.

Source F   Heresy

On the 18th day of April, 1494, an old rotting heretic, weak minded from age, named Joan Broughton was burnt in Smithfield (London). This woman was four score years of age or more, and believed eight false teachings which I will not repeat, for hearing them is not pleasant or useful.

Kingsfold's 'Chronicles of London'

Source G Immorality

A monk and a nun in the stocks as a punishment for having an affair. Churchmen and women were supposed to be celibate – to have no sexual relationships.

Source H Thomas Wolsey

CARDINAL WOLSEY

Thomas Wolsey dressed as a cardinal

Born around 1472, the son of an Ipswich butcher, Thomas Wolsey became one of the richest men in England. Much of his wealth came from the Church. He was the Pope's representative in England. He had himself elected Abbot of St Albans, one of the richest monasteries in England, although he had never been a monk. Dressed in silk and velvet, Wolsey lived like a prince. He is described entering Westminster Hall, 'with two great crosses carried before him, with also two great pillars of silver, and his Sergeant-at-Arms with a great mace of silver gilt'.

Roger Lockyer, 'Tudor and Stuart Britain 1471-1714', 1964

Activities

1. Read Sources B, D and E. How might the Mass, relics and images help an ordinary Catholic feel closer to God?

2. The following criticisms of the Catholic Church were made around 1500.

   a) Churchmen were often more interested in power, money and women than in serving God.

   b) The Church came between the people and their God.

   c) There was too much superstition and not enough religion.

   d) The Catholic Church would not allow people to worship God in their own way. It could be very cruel.

   Which sources from A-H seem to support which statements? Explain why in each case.

3. Does the portrait of Thomas Wolsey (Source H) seem to show the man described by Roger Lockyer? Explain your answer.

Protestants

The problems in the Church led some Catholics to think again about how people should worship. In Europe a number of religious leaders (see the timeline, page 6), set up 'Protestant' - or rival churches.

One of the first was John Wycliffe in England, but his ideas did not spread abroad. The most famous was the German monk, Martin Luther. He believed that over the centuries the Catholic Church had changed for the worse. By the 1500s it was nothing like God wanted it to be. Most of Luther's ideas were not new, but he put the feelings of many into words and, in doing so, challenged the position of the Pope.

Protestant ideas spread to many countries in Europe. Their rulers were faced with a difficult choice – should they remain Catholic or change to the Protestant faith. Europe was divided by religion and faced many bloody and bitter wars.

The rise of Protestantism in the 16th century is known as the Reformation.

Source A   Protestant ideas

- Congregations should be involved in the services by singing hymns, listening to sermons and Bible readings. A good preacher was important. He could explain the Bible in a lively way to people who couldn't read.

- Each man and woman should try to make personal contact with God. They did not need the Pope or priests to do this for them.

- People should read the Bible for themselves. It should be their best friend and guide. More people should be taught to read. The Bible should be translated into their own language.

- Faith or belief was the most important thing for Christians. They did not need relics, statues and images to help them worship. These objects were treated like magic by too many ordinary people.

Source B

Jesus was a poor man from his birth to his death, turning away from worldly riches. But the Pope at Rome, from the time of his birth until he dies, tries to be worldly rich.

John Wycliffe, c.1360

Source D

If you have true faith that Christ is your saviour then at once you have a good God, for faith leads you to God and opens his heart. Faith is enough for a Christian. He does not need any works (church services). He is definitely free from all (Catholic) commandments and laws.

Martin Luther, 1515

Source E

The report of these events has spread throughout all Germany. It stirs up the minds of all Germans against the Pope. The evils must be dealt with or I very much fear that they will spread far and wide and become unstoppable.

Alfonso de Valdes, a Spanish Catholic, writing in 1520 about the impact of Martin Luther's ideas

Source C

These pictures are copied from a painting in a book made in Bohemia, part of modern Czechoslovakia, in 1572. They show Wycliffe striking a spark and Luther holding a burning torch.

Activities

1. Look at Source A and pages 8-9. What might a Catholic say to persuade Protestants that their ideas are wrong? Write a short speech with the title, 'An answer to heresy'.

2. Many people who became Protestants could not read. Draw a picture to illustrate the ideas in Source B.

3. Look at Source C. What is the artist trying to show?

4. Read Source D. Why was Luther seen as a threat to the Pope and the Catholic Church?

5. Read Source E.

   a) Why is Alphonso de Valdes so worried?

   b) If you were an adviser to the Pope, what would you suggest to stop the spread of Protestant ideas?

The King's Reformation

Henry VIII is the key figure in the Reformation in England and Wales. In 1527 Henry wanted a divorce from his wife Catherine of Aragon. She had given birth to a daughter, Mary, but was unable to have any more children. To Henry a male heir was vital to keep his family on the throne. When the Pope refused to grant a divorce he was furious.

Source A

Henry used Parliament to bring in new laws to weaken the power of the Church.

1532 The Annates Act stopped English bishops and abbots paying any taxes to the Pope.

1533 The Appeals Act stopped any English law cases being judged by the Pope in Rome.

1534 The Treason Act made death the punishment for anyone who said Henry was a tyrant or a heretic.

1534 The Act of Supremacy made the monarch Supreme Head of the Church in England, so breaking the link with the Pope.

Source C

As monasteries were closed down a list was made of moveable goods such as animals, hay and grain, much of which was sold locally. Gold, silver and jewels were sent to the Master of the King's Jewel House. The lead on the roofs was melted down and sold. This could be very valuable. Lead from St Osyth Priory in Essex was valued at the enormous sum of £1044. The bells were also melted down. For the next two centuries monastery buildings became quarries for the local inhabitants for miles around.

Michael Reed, 'The Age of Exuberance 1500-1700', 1986

Henry now decided the Catholic Church was too powerful. It must be made to obey him in his kingdom, not the Pope. In 1533, Henry persuaded the Archbishop of Canterbury to grant his divorce. He then moved on to strip the Church of the influence it had built up over centuries. The Catholic Church in England was turned into the Church of England with Henry as its head.

Between 1536 and 1539 Henry closed all the monasteries and nunneries in England and Wales. Historians call this the 'dissolution of the monasteries'. The monks and nuns had taken vows to obey the Pope and were seen as a threat to royal power. Their buildings were amongst the finest in the country and they controlled vast areas of land – almost a quarter of the kingdom. The king was eager to seize these riches to pay for the high cost of defending his realm.

Henry wasn't interested in Protestant ideas. He wanted the way people worshipped to stay the same, but with him in control. Yet many ordinary people were deeply upset. They had to make the painful choice between loyalty to Henry or loyalty to the Pope.

Source B

ingot

stamp

2   0   2 Cm.

20   0   20 Cm.

A lead ingot, carrying the royal stamp, found by archaeologists at Rievaulx Abbey, North Yorkshire.

Source D   Fountains Abbey

The well preserved ruins of Fountains Abbey, North Yorkshire

Source E

I did object to the closing of the monasteries and so did all the country because the abbeys in the north gave great alms (money) to poor men and served God well. The abbeys were one of the beauties of this realm to all men and were great maintainers and builders of sea walls, bridges and highways.

Robert Aske, 1537. Aske led the Pilgrimage of Grace, a rebellion in the north of England against Henry's attacks on the Catholic Church. He was executed in York.

Source F

There was little sign of growing hatred amongst ordinary people towards the Catholic Church. Wills in the early 16th century show English men and women pouring gifts into their parish churches. An example is Etheldreda Swan, a woman by no means rich, who lived in a village in Cambridgeshire. A shilling (1s) was a large amount of money at this time.

The last will and testament of Etheldreda Swan

For the high altar	*1s*
For the bells	*1s*
For torches	*1s*
For church repairs	*1s 8d*
For Our Lady's light	*13s 4d*
For my own funeral	*1s 2d*

J. J. Scarisbrick, 'The Reformation and the English People', 1984

Activities

1. Why did Henry VIII attack the Catholic Church?

2. Look at Source A. How might a Catholic bishop feel about these laws? Write a letter to the king explaining your worries. Begin, 'Your Majesty, I humbly beseech you to think again'.

3. Most of the monasteries from the Middle Ages are now in ruins. Using Sources B, C and D, explain why.

4. Englishmen and women wanted the Reformation. Do Sources E and F support this statement? Give reasons for your answer.

5. A catchphrase or slogan can sometimes help a cause. Think of a slogan for the Pilgrimage of Grace, Source E.

Puritans

After Henry VIII's death, his nine year old son Edward became king. Edward's advisers moved England further towards Protestantism. A new official Protestant prayer book with services in English was published in 1549. When Edward died in 1553, his Catholic stepsister Mary became queen. She was determined to make England Catholic again and the Pope was once more made head of the Church. However, Mary reigned for only five years and her stepsister Elizabeth restored the Protestant Church. Catholics were seen as a threat and persecuted – see the Focus on page 7.

Conflict between Catholics and Protestants was not the only religious division. Protestants argued fiercely amongst themselves. Some saw the Church of England as little better than the Catholic Church. The bishops were still in control only now they were given their jobs by the king and queen, rather than by the Pope. Monarchs and archbishops laid down the rules for worship and published official prayer books. There seemed little room for freedom of worship.

Some Protestants challenged the Church of England. They were called Puritans because they wished to 'purify' the Church. They based their faith on the words of the Bible. They believed in a very simple form of worship and wanted to get rid of everything that reminded them of the Catholic Church – the stained glass windows, ornate statues, fine tapestries and paintings, churchmen dressed in splendid clothes and elaborate ceremonies and rituals.

During the Commonwealth (1649-1660) the Puritans tried to force their views on the rest of the country. They saw many sports and entertainments as evil. Bull baiting and cock fighting were banned, theatres closed. Parts of the traditional Christmas were seen as sinful and soldiers patrolled houses to pull Christmas roasts from the oven.

Source A

When Queen Elizabeth came to the Crown the nation became divided into three great factions (groups), the Papist (Catholic), the State-Protestant (Church of England) and the more strictly religious people, who afterwards were branded with the name of Puritan.

Lucy Hutchinson's biography of her husband Colonel John Hutchinson

Source B   A Puritan pamphlet

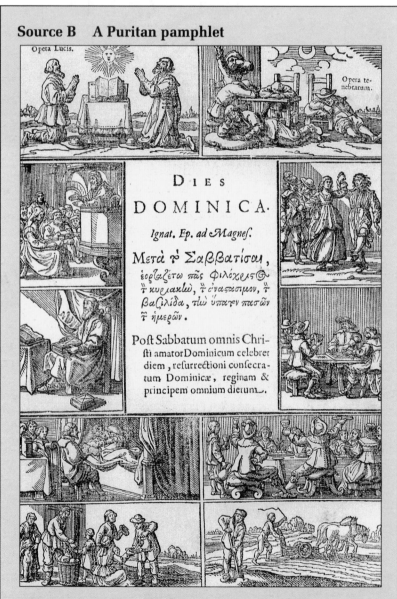

A Puritan pamphlet called *The Lord's Day*, published in 1639. It gives a Puritan view of how people were supposed to behave on Sunday. On the left are the 'Works of Light' and on the right, the 'Works of Darkness'.

Source C

Speech bubbles in image: "Keep out, you come not here;" / "O Sir, I bring good cheere." / "Old Christmas welcome; Do not fear."

From a pamphlet published in 1653. Father Christmas is driven out of town by a Puritan.

Source D

In the village where I lived the Common Prayer was read briefly. The rest of Sunday until it was almost dark, except eating time, was spent dancing under a maypole and a great tree, not far from my father's door. We could not read the scripture in our family without the noise of the tabor (small drum) and pipe in the street.

Many times I wished to join them. But when I heard them call my father Puritan, it did much to turn me against them.

Richard Baxter writing in 1664 about his childhood in a Shropshire village

Source E

Swearing is punishable by a fine of three shillings and fourpence or three hours in the stocks. All oaths, 'As God is my Witness', 'Upon my Life' and such like shall be so punished.

London byelaws, 1656

Source F

Fined Lucy, servant girl, 10 shillings for cleaning mistress's house on the Sabbath.

To be put in the stocks for three hours, Frances, for mending a dress upon the Lord's Day.

Bridewell Parish, 1655

Checklist

- Britain was a Catholic country in 1500, but a century later was Protestant.
- Protestants wanted to bring in new ideas about how to worship. Martin Luther was the most important Protestant thinker in Europe.
- Henry VIII brought the Reformation to England and Wales because he wanted to control the Church.
- Protestants argued amongst themselves. Puritans wanted to continue the Reformation by reforming the Church of England.

Activities

1. Read Source A. What 'faction' do you think Lucy belonged to? How can you tell from the words she uses?

2. Look at Source B. Why are the pictures on the right called the 'Works of Darkness'?

3. Read Source D.
   a) Why does Richard want to join the other villagers?
   b) How do you think the villagers said the word 'Puritan'? Try saying it out loud.
   c) What effect did this have on Richard?

4. Sources E and F are rules passed by Puritans during the Commonwealth. Many people felt the Puritans were too strict. Do you agree? Give reasons for your answer.

5. What message do you think the artist is trying to give in Source C?

The Tudor family
(dates show years of reign)

Henry VII (1485-1509)

He becomes the first member of the Tudor family to rule England.

Henry VIII (1509-1547)

Henry breaks with the Catholic Church. He makes the monarch the head of the Church of England.

Edward VI (1547-1553)

As Henry's only son he becomes ruler of England before his elder sisters, Mary and Elizabeth.
As a boy king (he died when he was only 16) the government was in the hands of powerful nobles throughout his reign.

Mary (1553-1558)

Mary becomes queen after the death of her stepbrother Edward. She tries to make England a Catholic country once again.

Elizabeth I (1558-1603)

Elizabeth becomes queen after the death of her stepsister Mary. She makes England a Protestant country once again. She never marries and has no children. She is the last member of the Tudor family to rule England.

Themes

Today it is Parliament that governs the country. The monarch has little say in government. Members of Parliament are elected. The political party which wins most seats in Parliament forms the government.

In 1500 the situation was very different. Only the monarch had the right to rule. Parliament only met when the monarch instructed it to do so. It only discussed those matters which the monarch ordered it to discuss.

During the reigns of the Tudor monarchs Parliament began to flex its muscles and grow stronger. As Parliament became stronger, the monarch became weaker.

Religion played an important part in these changes. Monarchs and their subjects were expected to have the same religion. In England the official religion became Protestant. Catholics, whether they were subjects or rulers, were looked upon with at best suspicion, at worst as traitors.

This chapter asks the following questions.

- How powerful was the monarchy?
- What part did Parliament play in the government of the country?
- What part did religion play in the changes in the way Britain was governed?

We begin with Thomas Cranmer's speech on the power of the monarch made during Henry VIII's reign.

Focus Activities

1. From where does the monarch get his or her right to rule?
2. Under what circumstances could you disobey the monarch?
3. Why did Cranmer think that his view of government was a good one?
4. Why might Catholics reject the right of Henry to be king?

Kings made by God

Thomas Cranmer, Archbishop of Canterbury, thought carefully. He was due to meet Henry and make a speech about the power of kings. When the king had wanted a divorce from his first wife Catherine, Cranmer had supported him. When Henry broke away from the Catholic Church Cranmer had backed him.

Henry could be crafty, brutal, selfish and ungrateful. Yet he was the king. But were there limits to the power of kings? Archbishop Cranmer cleared his throat and began to speak.

'Almighty God has created everything that exists in heaven, on earth and in the waters. He has created everything in the most perfect order. On earth he has made kings, princes, with other noble people under them all in good order. And he has created the lower people to serve them. Where there is no order, there is quarrelling, fighting and sin. Let us always remember that the high power and authority of kings are the laws of God.

Yet there are some circumstances in which we do not have to obey kings. If they command us to do anything against God's words we must obey God.'

Thomas Cranmer (1489-1556)

Henry made Thomas Cranmer his Archbishop of Canterbury. Cranmer agreed with Luther and led the Reformation in England. During the reign of Henry's son, Edward VI, he made changes to the Church of England which moved it even further from the Catholic Church. In 1549 Cranmer published a new Protestant prayer book (written by himself) with services in English.

During the reign of Henry's eldest daughter Mary, Cranmer's beliefs were put to the test. Mary was a Catholic and determined to restore the Catholic Church in England. She demanded that Cranmer obey her and publicly confess that he was wrong to support the Protestant Church. He refused and was put on trial and burned at the stake as a heretic.

Henry VIII and Parliament

The main duty of Parliament was to grant money from taxes for the monarch. Parliament did not meet often, but during Henry VIII's reign there was a dramatic increase in the length of time that Parliaments were in session and the number of laws they passed.

Henry VII, who reigned for 24 years, called seven Parliaments which sat for a total of 37 months. Henry VIII, who reigned for 38 years, called nine Parliaments which met for a total of 170 months and passed hundreds of laws. This increase is partly explained by the need for so many laws to bring about the Reformation in England and partly by the policy of Henry's adviser Thomas Cromwell. He saw Parliament as a useful way of making sure important people backed the king.

Henry and Cromwell made sure that they had a number of loyal followers in Parliament.

As a result of its growing influence, Parliament became an accepted part of the government of the country. This partnership worked well when monarch and Parliament were in agreement.

Source A   Henry VIII

We are at our most royal when we come together with one Parliament as one body. Any threat to one part of the body is a threat to us all.

Henry VIII, 1543

Source C

An Act of 1483 stated that it was illegal for the monarch to order taxes without the agreement of Parliament.

Source D

The discussions in the English Parliament are free and unrestricted. The Crown has no power to stop free discussion or control the votes of members.

Henry VIII to the Pope, 1529

Source B

Things that the monarch wanted to make into laws were known as 'bills'. They were usually introduced into Parliament by the monarch's advisers.

A bill would be discussed in the House of Commons. Sometimes changes were made to the bill.

The bill was then discussed in the House of Lords. Changes might be made there.

The bill would then become law if the monarch agreed. If the monarch refused then the bill would not become law. The monarch could also pass laws (called proclamations) without Parliament but this was very rare.

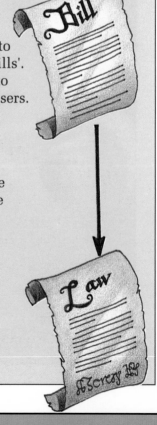

Source E

Henry used threats when he wanted to get his own way. In 1532 he wanted to stop landholders passing on land to their sons and avoiding the tax payable to the king. He ordered a group of MPs to meet him and told them:

'You should not oppose me – I am your sovereign lord king. If you will not come to an agreement, I will use all the powers of the law against you.'

Parliament agreed to Henry's demands.

Source F

In 1529 and again in 1532 Parliament refused to accept a bill which gave the king the right to claim an inheritance tax on land.

Source H

In 1536 Thomas Cromwell, Henry's chief adviser, wanted two men to be elected as MPs at Canterbury. The sheriff said the election had already taken place, but Cromwell refused to accept this. Cromwell ordered the sheriff:

'To hold a new election and elect those I want. Should you fail to do so you will suffer the king's displeasure.'

Cromwell's two men were elected soon after.

Source G

Henry VIII opening Parliament, 1523

Activities

Read the section introduction and the sources carefully and use them to answer these questions.

1. List the strengths and weaknesses of the monarch and Parliament.
2. Why did the monarch find Parliament useful?
3. How did Members of Parliament use their influence on the monarch?
4. How did the monarch make sure that he usually got his own way with Parliament?
5. Why do you think the king opened Parliament?

Queen and Parliament

Elizabeth I called ten Parliaments in her 45 year reign. They met for a total of 218 months. She needed Parliament to pass laws against Catholics and to grant her money. Parliament often sat for long periods of time. MPs used this as an opportunity to increase their influence.

Like her father Henry, Elizabeth used a variety of ways to make sure she got what she wanted. She had her key advisers elected to Parliament. She used flattery and persuasion and, as a last resort, imprisoned MPs if she felt they went too far. Furthermore, she could call or close down Parliament when she wanted to and scrap laws if she did not like them. She used these powers and gave way only rarely.

Source A   Members of Parliament

House of Lords

Peers (noblemen), abbots and bishops

House of Commons

Knights of the shire and burgesses

Members of the House of Lords were not elected. They were there because they were rich and powerful. Knights from the counties and burgesses from the towns were elected to the Commons. Only rich people were allowed to vote – most people took no part in elections.

Source B   Member of Parliament

Parliament is useful to me because:

- It shows how important I am and the queen might choose me as an adviser.

- I can pass on the views of people in my part of the country.

- I can persuade the queen to limit the amount of taxes she wants us to pay.

- I can have some say in how the country is run.

Queen Elizabeth

Parliament is useful to me because:

- It helps me to pass laws – if Parliament agrees then it shows that the whole country agrees with me.

- I sometimes need more money to run the country and MPs will help me to raise taxes.

- They give me advice and information.

- I can explain why I want certain laws passed.

Source C   Elizabeth's Parliaments

Dates	Reasons for calling Parliament
1559	1. To organise the Church of England as a Protestant Church. 2. To grant taxes.
1563-67	1. To discuss a rebellion in Scotland. 2. To grant taxes. 3. A Protestant rebellion in France - should England help the rebels? 4. To grant further taxes.
1571	1. Mary, Queen of Scots, escapes imprisonment by her own people in Scotland who had rebelled against her. She flees to England in 1568 to ask for help. What should England do? 2. To grant taxes.
1572-83	1. Catholic plots to assassinate Elizabeth. Laws passed against Catholics. 2. To grant taxes. 3. Catholic plots. Tighter laws passed against Catholics. 4. To grant further taxes. 5. Harsh laws passed against Catholics. 6. To grant further taxes.
1584-85	1. Severe laws passed against anyone plotting against the Queen. 2. To grant taxes.
1586-87	1. New harsh laws against Catholics. 2. Some grumbling about new taxes, but finally granted.
1589	1. War with Spain. 2. Double taxes granted.
1593	1. War in Ireland. 2. Triple taxes granted.
1597-98	1. War in Ireland. 2. Triple taxes granted.
1601	1. For Elizabeth to announce the next ruler of England after her death. 2. Triple taxes granted.

Source D   Freedom of speech

Elizabeth and her Parliament often disagreed about freedom of speech. For example, she was furious when Parliament discussed changes to the Church of England in 1587. She imprisoned five MPs and ordered an immediate end to the discussion. Later in her reign she was careful to make it clear that MPs were punished for things they said outside and not inside Parliament. However, she still tried to limit their freedom of speech within Parliament.

'For freedom of speech her Majesty commands me to say that no man should be afraid to say yes or no to bills. But he is not there to speak of all things that come into his mind or to suggest new religions and governments. She said that no monarch fit to rule would allow anything so stupid.'

The Lord Keeper's reply to a petition from Parliament for freedom of speech , 1593

Activities

1. Who did Parliament represent (Source A)? Give reasons for your answer.

2. Read Source B. What disagreements might Elizabeth have with MPs?

3. a) According to Source C what were the main problems faced by Elizabeth's government?

   b) Wars were very expensive. What evidence for this is provided by Source C?

4. Why was the question of freedom of speech in Parliament so important both to MPs and Elizabeth? (Source D)

The Privy Council

Parliament only met when Elizabeth wanted it to. This meant that the day-to-day business of government was carried out by the queen and her closest advisers.

Elizabeth chose a small group of men from her court to become her closest advisers. These men were known as Privy (private) Councillors. There were between 12 and 20 Privy Councillors when the full council met, but quite often she consulted only 5 or 6.

Source A

Elizabeth was against executing Mary, Queen of Scots, but the Privy Councillors were for it. Cecil, her chief adviser, by much persuasion and strong reason, guided her majesty in the drawing-up of the document of execution.

Calendar of State Papers, 1588

Source B   Queen Elizabeth I

Elizabeth's government went to great lengths to make sure she looked her best in paintings. The Privy Council had a standard picture of her made which all painters had to copy. This portrait was painted very late in her reign.

Source C

Her wisest and best councillors were often confused about what Elizabeth had decided, because she made her decisions in great secret.

When she smiled it was pure sunshine, and everyone tried to bathe in it if they could. Once she sent a letter to the Earl of Essex which was so fierce that he fainted and he became so swelled up that, throwing himself upon his bed, all the buttons of his doublet broke away as though they had been cut with a knife.

Sir John Harrington, godson of Queen Elizabeth, 1602

Activities

1. What do Sources A, C and D tell us about the relationship between Elizabeth and her Privy Councillors?

2. If Elizabeth's temper was so bad, why did her Privy Councillors put up with her? (Sources C and D)

3. What was the purpose in having one standard picture of Elizabeth which all painters were meant to copy? (Source B)

Source D

Her temper was so bad that no Privy Councillor dared mention any business to her. When Cecil, her chief adviser, tried to do so, she told him that she had been strong enough to lift him out of the dirt and she could easily throw him back again.

Calendar of State Papers, 1584

William Cecil, 1520-1598

Elizabeth's most important adviser was William Cecil. He served Elizabeth first as Secretary of State (chief adviser) then as Lord Treasurer (in charge of the finances of the country). He was a sort of Tudor prime minister. However he was not elected but chosen by the queen.

Source A

I give you this important job on my Privy Council so that you may serve me and my realm. This judgement I have of you, that you will not take bribes and that you will tell me your honest opinion no matter what you personally think.

Elizabeth to William Cecil, 1559

Source B   William Cecil, Lord Burghley

Source C

William Cecil was made Secretary of State, then Master of the Court of Wards*, and then Lord Treasurer, for he was a man of great ability. He achieved great success not by the sword but by the information he received from his spies in England and in foreign countries. He was able to unlock the secrets of the Queen's enemies.

Sir Robert Naunton, 1641

*The Court of Wards looked after the property of children whose wealthy parents had died. Cecil made a lot of money from this position.

Source D

The most important man in the Privy Council is William Cecil. He is a clever, false, lying man. He is a Protestant heretic and such a fool as to think that all the Catholic princes joined together could not harm his Queen. He is very arrogant with foreign ambassadors.

State Papers - a description of William Cecil by the Spanish Ambassador, 1586

Activities

1. a) What was Elizabeth looking for in a chief adviser? (Source A)

    b) Why was she looking for these qualities?

2. Why would many courtiers be keen to be Elizabeth's chief adviser? (Source C)

3. a) Source C gives a very different opinion of William Cecil than Source D. Suggest reasons for this.

    b) Because the sources are different does this mean that one of the sources is incorrect?

4. Look closely at Source B. What do you think the painter is trying to tell us about William Cecil?

The Queen's Finances

Monarchs were expected to pay for the cost of running the country from their own income which came from the land they owned, and from customs duties. There was never enough money, however, and kings and queens continually asked Parliament to grant new taxes. The biggest drain on money was when England had to fight wars. Things were made even worse for Elizabeth because it was a time of rapidly rising prices – they rose far more quickly than the queen's income.

Source A   A gold sovereign (£1)

Prices doubled during Elizabeth's reign. Between 1558 and 1603 the value of a sovereign fell by half.

Source B

INCOME		EXPENDITURE	
Where the money came from for the queen's government (1600)	£	How the money was spent (1600)	£
Fines collected in the law courts	10 000	Queen's personal spending	2 000
Rent from people living on the queen's lands	60 000	Payments to servants	4 000
Payments from the Chancellor	4 000	Household expenses	8 000
Sale of queen's lands	4 000	Payments for courtiers' clothes	4 000
Customs duties from ports	80 000	Payments for looking after the royal jewels and treasures	6 000
Customs duties from wine	24 000	Expenses for ambassadors	4 000
Payments for giving people trading licences	5 000	Looking after royal buildings	5 000
Fines against Catholics	7 000	The navy	17 000
Payments from church taxes	20 000	Payment for small private army	6 400
Taxes granted by Parliament	160 000	Looking after castles and forts	6 000
		Payment of judges	1 600
	374 000	War in Ireland	320 000
		Help for Dutch rebels fighting against Spain	25 000
		Pensions given out by the queen	26 000
			435 000

Activities

1. Look at Source A. What problems might this have caused for Elizabeth?

2. Read Source B.

   a) What is the queen's main item of income?

   b) What is her main item of expenditure?

   c) Compare the totals of income and expenditure. What financial difficulty did she have?

   d) How does this help to explain why Elizabeth needed Parliament?

Justices of the Peace

Elizabeth and her Parliament could make laws but how could they make sure that they were obeyed throughout the country?

In every county of England the queen had a personal official called the Lord Lieutenant. He was helped by Justices of the Peace (JPs) who had a huge number of jobs to do. Their main job was to make sure the law was obeyed, but they were also responsible for making sure repairs were made to roads and bridges and giving licences to ale-houses.

JPs were not paid but it was an important job. They were chosen from the ranks of the well-off local gentry.

Source A   From a diary kept by William Lombarde, JP

1581
8 Aug.   Granted ale-house licence to Roger Meane on payment of £10.
23 Aug.   Investigated eight confidence tricksters. Sent them to gaol.

1583
23 Feb.   Examined witnesses about the poisoning of William Brightside by Thomas Heyward and Pamel. Pamel had been William's wife but was now married to Heyward.
20 July   I wrote to all parts of the county to tell them of a tax for the gaol and house of correction.
30 Sept.   Fined a Catholic for refusing to attend the Church of England. Several warnings had been given.

Source B   Punishments

Source C

If he is judged to be a vagabond, he is to be whipped and a hole burnt in the lobe of his ear with a hot iron. If he is found guilty again his other ear will be burnt and he will be made a servant. If he is found guilty a third time he will be condemned to death.

William Harrison, 'The Description of England', 1586

Activities

1. Why did Elizabeth's government need Justices of the Peace? (Source A)
2. Justices of the Peace were not paid. Why did they accept the position?
3. Why were punishments so cruel?

Mary Queen of Scots

Elizabeth and her government faced their most serious threat when Mary, Elizabeth's cousin, fled across the border into England in 1568. She had angered her Scottish subjects with her outrageous behaviour. Her husband had been murdered and she was accused of being involved. Worse still, she married the man who had arranged her husband's death. Mary was Catholic and some Catholics in England believed that she should be the rightful Queen of England. Elizabeth imprisoned Mary but was at a loss to know what to do with her.

As plots were uncovered against Elizabeth's life, they all seemed to lead back to Mary. In 1586 Mary was finally caught red-handed in a plot. Parliament and the Privy Councillors urged Elizabeth to pass the death sentence on the Scots' queen. Elizabeth hesitated.

Source A

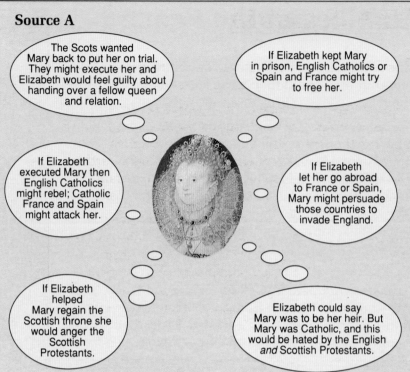

> The Scots wanted Mary back to put her on trial. They might execute her and Elizabeth would feel guilty about handing over a fellow queen and relation.

> If Elizabeth kept Mary in prison, English Catholics or Spain and France might try to free her.

> If Elizabeth executed Mary then English Catholics might rebel; Catholic France and Spain might attack her.

> If Elizabeth let her go abroad to France or Spain, Mary might persuade those countries to invade England.

> If Elizabeth helped Mary regain the Scottish throne she would anger the Scottish Protestants.

> Elizabeth could say Mary was to be her heir. But Mary was Catholic, and this would be hated by the English *and* Scottish Protestants.

Source B

The Queen's mind was greatly troubled. She signed a death warrant for Mary giving it to Davison, her secretary. The next day she changed her mind but it was too late. The warrant was delivered without the knowledge of the Queen and Mary was executed. William Davison was fined heavily and put in the Tower of London.

William Camden, 'Annales', 1615

Source C

On 8 February 1587 Mary, Queen of Scots, was executed at Fotheringay Castle. Three blows of the axe were needed to sever her head from her body.

Activities

1. Elizabeth wrote to Mary's son, King James VI of Scotland, after the execution of Mary:

   'My dearest brother,
   I want you to know the huge grief I feel for something which I did not want to happen and that I am innocent in the matter.'

   a) Why did Elizabeth write this letter?
   b) Do you agree with Elizabeth when she claims she is innocent? (Source B)

2. If you were Elizabeth, what would you have done with Mary (Source A)? Explain your answer.

The Armada

The execution of Mary, Queen of Scots, was the last straw for Philip II the Catholic King of Spain.

Spain had grown rich from the fabulous wealth of gold and silver she had found in the Americas. Many Spanish treasure ships were raided by English pirates with the full knowledge of Elizabeth. Furthermore, Elizabeth had helped the Dutch Protestant rebels fight against their Catholic Spanish rulers.

Philip decided that the Catholic Church must be avenged. In 1588 he sent a huge invasion fleet of 130 ships, carrying almost 25,000 men, on a crusade against the heretic Elizabeth. The plan was for the Armada to link up with Philip's general, the Duke of Parma, and an army of 17,000 Spanish soldiers in the Netherlands. Elizabeth and her Protestant government were to be swept from power.

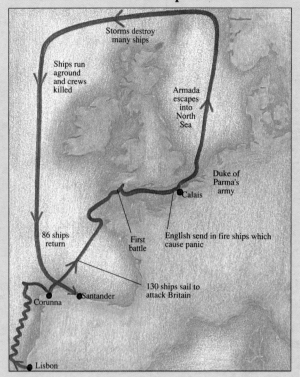

Source A   Route of the Spanish Armada

Source B

On Monday morning six fire ships were sent among the Spanish fleet. They were in great disorder and we had the wind and tide behind us. They lost a dozen or fourteen of their best ships and made haste to get away. On Thursday there was a mighty storm. Some ran ashore in Scotland and Ireland where they had their throats cut. Thus did God bless us and give us a great victory.

Sir Robert Carey, 1588. He sailed with the English fleet which fought the Armada.

Source C

In this difficult time, some beat it many times into the Queen's head, that the Spaniards were not to be as much feared as the Catholics in England. For safety, they advised the heads of the chief Catholics should be chopped off on a false charge. The Queen thought this cruel advice and did no more than imprison some.

William Camden, 'Annales', 1615

Activities

1. Why did Philip decide to invade England?

2. a) Why did Elizabeth have to be careful about her treatment of English Catholics? (Source C)
   b) How does this source show Elizabeth is in charge of her government?

3. a) How was the Spanish Armada defeated according to the English? (Source B)
   b) How might the Spanish explain their defeat?

Checklist

- The Tudor monarchs were very powerful but they needed advisers and officials to help them run the country.

- Monarchs needed Parliament particularly to help raise money through taxes.

- When MPs were called to Parliament they used the opportunity to increase their influence.

4 KING AND PARLIAMENT

1603	James VI of Scotland becomes James I, King of England.
1605	The gunpowder plot. A Catholic plot to blow up James and his Parliament fails.
1611	The Authorised (official) version of the Bible is printed. This was the work of 47 Protestant scholars.
1618	James allows his favourite, the Duke of Buckingham, to rule the country.
1620	Some strict Protestants called Puritans leave England for America on a ship called the *Mayflower*.
1625	James dies and his son Charles becomes king.
1628	Parliament wants Charles to sign the Petition of Right. This would make the king less powerful.
1629	Charles rules without Parliament.
1640	When a Scottish army invades England he calls a Parliament to raise money to defend himself.
1642–1649	War between Parliament and the king.

CIVIL WAR

1649	Charles I is executed by order of Parliament.
1649–1660	Oliver Cromwell, General of the Parliamentary armies, rules Britain. Britain has no monarch. It is a republic.

Themes

In 1603 James VI of Scotland, the son of Mary Queen of Scots, became King of England. He was the first of a new family of kings and queens, called the Stuarts, who ruled Britain from 1603 to 1714.

During the reigns of the Stuart kings Parliament demanded more power. Merchants, particularly, were growing in wealth and wanted a larger say in the running of the country. The Stuart kings tried to resist these changes.

The conflict got worse during the reign of Charles I, James's son, and eventually broke out into civil war. A civil war is a war fought between people who belong to the same country.

This chapter looks at the following questions.

- Why did Parliament and the Stuart kings quarrel with one another?

- Why did civil war break out and what did each side believe it was fighting for?

In our opening Focus, Parliament has won the civil war and King Charles I is about to be executed. The year is 1649.

Focus Activities

You are a member of the crowd. You feel sick and fear you may faint at what you have seen. Staggering to a nearby inn, you sink into a comfortable seat and ask yourself these questions. What are the answers?

1. Why was the crowd so silent?

2. Why did some dip their handkerchiefs in Charles's blood?

3. Why was Charles I executed in public?

4. Why was there such a large crowd and so many troops?

5. Why were the executioner and his assistant disguised?

The King must die!

It was nearly two o'clock on a bitterly cold January afternoon – January 30th, 1649. Today a king was to die.

Colonel Francis Hacker, commander in charge of the royal prisoner, knocked for the last time on the king's door. Charles, King of England, Scotland and Ireland calmly waited. Sometimes he sat in silence, sometimes talking to Bishop Juxon. He had said farewell to his children Henry and Elizabeth earlier and was now awaiting the final call. Charles and James, his eldest sons, had escaped and were now safely abroad.

Colonel Hacker spoke in a whisper to the king that the time had come. Hacker led the way, the king followed. Charles passed through the hall of Whitehall Palace and out on to the scaffold upon which rested the execution block. The scaffold was draped in black cloth and everywhere, but everywhere, there were soldiers.

Charles looked towards his place of execution. Four pegs had been driven into the wood to fasten the king should he put up a struggle. The executioner and his assistant were masked and heavily disguised in false beards and wigs.

Troops on horseback ringed the scaffold keeping the crowd back at a safe distance. People filled the streets and gazed in mute silence.

Charles took a small piece of crumpled paper from his pocket and unfolded it. His last words were no more and than a whisper.

'All the world knows that I never did begin a war with Parliament... I believe it is evil men who have been the cause of all this bloodshed... I die a Christian of the Church of England... I will say no more.'

He took off his jewels and handed them to Bishop Juxon repeating one final word to him, 'Remember'. He removed his doublet but replaced his cloak to guard against the bitter wind that blew off the Thames. The king stood for a moment, raised his eyes, prayed in silence, slipped off his cloak and lay down with his neck on the block. The executioner bent down and brushed the king's hair to one side to give a clean cut of the neck. Thinking he was about to strike, Charles said, 'Wait for the sign'.

A fearful silence fell upon the crowd. The king stretched out his hand and in the same instant one blow of the axe severed his head from his body. A groan ran like a wave through the crowd as the king's head, dripping with blood, was lifted and shown to them. The crowd surged forward. Some dipped handkerchiefs in the royal blood, but were soon pushed back as the streets were cleared by troopers.

The king's head is cut from his body.

James I and Parliament

In 1603 James VI of Scotland, son of Mary Queen of Scots, became King James I of England. He was the nearest living relative to Queen Elizabeth.

Things looked good for James. He was already an experienced king, having ruled Scotland from 1584. He had been brought up a Protestant, had replaced a woman ruler, and already had two sons to follow him when he died.

Although James ruled until 1625, things went from bad to worse with Parliament. Part of the problem was James himself, part was the growing strength of Parliament and its demands for greater power.

Source A   An opinion of James I as King of Scotland

He is well educated, has remarkable intelligence and a high opinion of himself. His manners are crude. He loves hunting and will go on the chase for six hours without stopping. His body is feeble, yet he is not delicate.

I have noticed in him three weaknesses that may prove harmful to government. He does not realise how short of money he is; he relies too much on favourites and takes no notice of what people think; he is too lazy about government. Such weaknesses can be excused of someone so young, but I fear they may become habits.

De Fontenoy, the French Ambassador to the Scottish Court, 1586

Source C

I am surprised that my ancestors should have allowed Parliament to exist.

James's opinion of Parliament, 1617

Source B

The state of monarchy is the highest power on earth, for kings are appointed rulers on earth by God himself.

James's opinion of the monarchy, 1609

Source D   James's favourite – George Villiers, the Duke of Buckingham

George Villiers

These were only some of his titles – George, Duke, Marquis and Earl of Buckingham, Earl of Coventry, Grand Admiral of the Kingdom of England and Ireland.

James was very fond of George Villiers and gave him great powers. From 1618 onwards Villiers more or less ruled the kingdom. He wasted money and dragged England and Scotland into pointless wars with France and Spain, prevented other men from rising to power and quarrelled bitterly with Parliament. He continued in favour with Charles I, until his assassination in 1628 at the hands of one of his unpaid soldiers.

'No man, in any age, nor I believe in any country or nation, rose in so short a time to so much greatness of honour, fame and fortune, for no reason other than the beauty of his person.'
Edward Hyde, Earl of Clarendon, 1625

When Members of Parliament complained about Buckingham, James replied (1621), 'You may be sure that I love Buckingham more than anyone else, and more than all of you put together'.

Source E   Quarrels with the Puritans

A Puritan cartoon attacking the Catholic Church

The Puritans hoped that James, who had been brought up as a strict Protestant, would change the Church of England to fit their beliefs. They felt it was far too similar to the Catholic Church. They saw ceremonies like confirmation, special clothes for priests and bowing at the name of Christ during services as hangovers from the Catholic Church.

A special meeting to discuss the Church of England was arranged at Hampton Court in 1604. The Puritans were disappointed. James was happy with the Church of England as it was and told them flatly:

'If I mean to live with Puritans I will go to live in Scotland. You must obey me or I will chase you from this land, or else do worse.'

Some Puritans left for Holland and America. Others stayed and got themselves into Parliament to try to alter the laws governing the Church of England.

Source F   Foreign policy

James wished his son Charles to marry a Spanish princess. He tried to make a good impression with the Spaniards by having Sir Walter Raleigh, who had captured Spanish treasure ships, executed as they wished.

Parliament wanted nothing to do with such schemes. Spain was England's traditional enemy and Catholic. Parliament wanted war, not an alliance. James was furious. He refused to call any more Parliaments and went ahead with his marriage scheme.

George Villiers, Duke of Buckingham, and James's son Charles disguised themselves and went to woo the Spanish princess. The Spaniards were shocked at such an adventure and the marriage plans came to nothing. Villiers felt insulted and on his return to England persuaded Parliament to declare war on Spain.

Parliament was only too delighted to grant money for the war. A few months later James died, leaving George Villiers and Charles to carry on the war.

Activities

1. How might the character of James make him a bad ruler? (Source A)

2. What did James believe about:
   (i)   Parliament
   (ii) the monarchy?
   (Sources B and C)

3. There were several other reasons why Parliament and the king did not get on well (Sources D, E and F). Explain these reasons using the following headings:

   FAVOURITES
   PURITANS
   FOREIGN POLICY

4. What do you think the cartoon in Source E is saying? (The man in the cloak is the Pope.)

Charles I and Parliament

Charles proved no better than his father at ruling with Parliament. Firstly, the Spanish war went badly. Arriving in Cadiz, the English sailors got drunk and hastily retreated when attacked. Parliament blamed Charles's favourite, the hated George Villiers, Duke of Buckingham, for this defeat.

Secondly, George Villiers seemed to have as much control over Charles as he had over James. When Villiers was assassinated by one of his unpaid soldiers, the king married a French Catholic princess, Henrietta Maria. She had a great influence upon him. Parliament resented this.

Thirdly, Parliament refused many of Charles's demands for taxes. The king was forced to borrow by threats and promises. Parliament finally granted Charles a small amount of money when he agreed to a list of demands known as the Petition of Right (1628). Charles promptly ignored this agreement, imprisoned several MPs who had led the Petition and began raising his own taxes without Parliament's permission.

By 1629 Charles was so dissatisfied with Parliament that he ruled for eleven years without calling MPs to meet. This made his opponents, particularly the Puritans, very angry. During this period he relied heavily on two close advisers.

Thomas Wentworth, the Earl of Strafford, helped Charles to rule Ireland. Wentworth did so with a rod of iron which earned him deep hatred in Ireland. Charles's other adviser, William Laud, Archbishop of Canterbury, was just as unpopular. He wanted the Puritans and the Scots to accept the Church of England. Parliament hated the king having favourites. MPs believed he should rule with them, and not just rely on favourites.

Crisis came in 1640. The Scots rebelled against William Laud's measures and a Scottish army occupied Northumberland and Durham. They refused to budge unless bribed by Charles. Charles had no money left and so called Parliament. Parliament realised it had the upper hand. On its orders William Laud was imprisoned and Strafford executed. MPs demanded that:

- Parliament must be called every three years.
- The king could only raise taxes with Parliament's permission.
- Parliament could only be dismissed if MPs agreed to go home.

Parliament then demanded that the king make the Church of England Puritan. Charles had had enough. Parliament and the king each began to raise armies. The Civil War began.

Source A   Charles I (1625-1649)

Source B

Reaction by Sir John Eliot, MP, to the news of the disastrous Spanish expedition of 1626:

Our honour is ruined, our ships are sunk, our men dead, not by chance, not by the sword, but by those we trusted. The lord (George Villiers) who led this is a cancer in the king's realm. By him come all our evils, in him we find the causes and on him must be the remedy.

Source C

Charles I's reaction to Sir John Eliot's speech:

Parliaments are altogether in my power for their calling, sitting and dissolutions. Therefore, as I find the fruits of them good or evil, they are to continue or not depending upon what I order.

Source D   The Petition of Right, 1628

1. No taxes without Parliament's permission.

2. Nobody to be imprisoned without a fair trial.

3. No royal troops to be billeted (forcing people to give board and lodgings to soldiers).

4. No martial law (the king could not use his army to run the country).

Source E   Cartoon from a Puritan pamphlet

In 1637 three Puritan writers were tried by a special king's court for criticising the Church of England. They were sentenced to be whipped, have their ears cut off, pay huge fines and be imprisoned for life. The large crowd who came to watch cheered the victims and booed the man punishing them. This cartoon, from a Puritan pamphlet, shows the Archbishop of Canterbury, William Laud, being served with the Puritans' ears.

Source F

John Pym, leader of the opposition to the king in the House of Commons, stated in 1640:

We must be more determined than we were in the last Parliament. We must not only sweep the House of Commons clean, but pull down all the cobwebs which hang in the top and corners, that they may not breed dust and make the House foul.

Activities

1. What do you think the artist wants to tell us about Charles I? (Source A)

2. Why does Sir John Eliot blame George Villiers and not the king? (Source B)

3. Why does Charles react in the way he does? (Source C)

4. How is Parliament trying to reduce the power of the king? (Source D)

5. How can you tell the cartoonist is on the side of the victims? (Source E)

6. How can you tell from John Pym's speech that he and his supporters are determined to oppose the king? (Source F)

The Civil War 1642-49

The Civil War not only split the country, it also split families. Brothers fought brothers, fathers fought sons. It was a war no one really wanted.

During the war about 100,000 British people were killed. (The population was about five million at this time.)

Most of Charles's support came from the Church of England, Catholics and many of the greatest landowners. Parliament controlled the navy and had the support of Puritans, smaller landowners and the wealthy merchants of London.

By 1646 Parliament won the day and the king was finally defeated. Charles bargained with Parliament in order to gain time.

In 1648 a Scottish army marched south to support Charles. He had made a secret deal with them. Cromwell, who had emerged as the leading Parliamentary general, was furious and demanded the king's execution.

Many Members of Parliament felt this was going too far and tried to dissuade Cromwell. He would have none of it and turned out all those MPs from the House of Commons who were not on his side. The eighty remaining MPs tried the king and condemned him to death. Oliver Cromwell was now in charge. Britain was a republic.

Source A

In this cartoon of 1642 Cavaliers and Roundheads are encouraging their dogs to attack one another.

The Cavaliers were supporters of Charles. They are dressed like Charles's courtiers, with long hair, grand clothes and plumed hats. The Roundheads were supporters of Parliament, and are shown with short, cropped hair and plainer clothes.

All Cavaliers and Roundheads did not look like this. They came from all social groups.

Source B

I do not like the quarrel and do heartily wish that the king would agree to what Parliament wants. But I have served the king nearly thirty years, and will not to do so bad a thing as to abandon him. I would rather lose my life, which I am sure I will do.

Sir Edmund Verney, a country gentleman from Claydon in Buckinghamshire. He was killed at the Battle of Edgehill, 1642.

Source C

Few of the common people cared much for either King or Parliament. They would have joined either side for pay and plunder.

Thomas Hobbes, Cavalier, 1643

Source D

I am afraid that the needy people of the whole kingdom will presently rise in mighty numbers and take over, ruining the nobility and the gentry.

John Hotham, Cavalier, 1648

Source E   Map of the Civil War

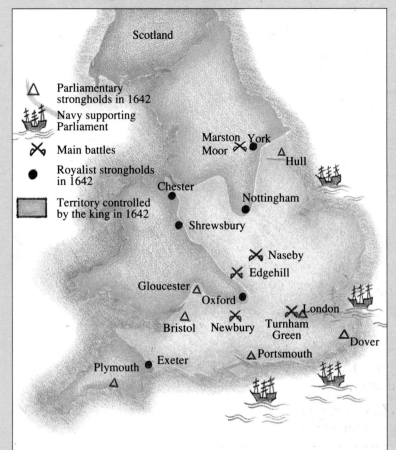

Scotland

△ Parliamentary strongholds in 1642

⛵ Navy supporting Parliament

⚔ Main battles

● Royalist strongholds in 1642

▢ Territory controlled by the king in 1642

Marston Moor ⚔ York
Hull △
Chester ●
Nottingham ●
Shrewsbury ●
⚔ Naseby
⚔ Edgehill
Gloucester △
Oxford ●
△ ⚔ London
Bristol   Newbury   Turnham Green ⚔
Dover △
Plymouth ● Exeter △ Portsmouth
△

Activities

1. a) If all Cavaliers and Roundheads did not look like the figures drawn in the cartoon, why has the artist drawn them like this? (Source A)

   b) Draw your own cartoons showing support for:
   (i) Parliament (ii) the king

2. Why do you think Sir Edmund Verney (Source B) fought for Charles I? List possible reasons and explain which was the most important.

3. What was John Hotham afraid of? (Source D)

4. Few people wanted war. What evidence from Sources B, C and D supports this statement?

5. What advantages did Parliament have? (Source E)

6. What do you think were the 'turning points' in the Civil War? (Source F)

Source F   Events of the Civil War

1642 The Battle of Edgehill – there was no clear winner although the king marched on London. He was stopped just outside London by a citizen army.

1643 The Royalist army again failed to reach London but they captured Bristol. Meanwhile Oliver Cromwell, a Huntingdon landowner and MP, was training his tough soldiers called Ironsides. Parliament lost two of its best leaders – John Hampden was killed in battle and John Pym died of cancer.

1644 The Scots joined forces with Parliament's army. The king was badly defeated at Marston Moor in Yorkshire. The north was lost to the king, but he still held the west and Oxford.

1645 Parliament organised the New Model Army under Sir Thomas Fairfax and Oliver Cromwell. They won a great victory at Naseby.

1646 The New Model Army captured the king's headquarters at Oxford. The king handed himself over to the Scots thinking that he might persuade them to fight for him. They gave him to Parliament in exchange for a large sum of money.

1648 Charles had made a secret deal with the Scots and a second civil war broke out. Cromwell quickly defeated the king.

1649 Charles was put on trial and executed.

Civil War armies

In the early years of the war, the king had the better of it. In particular, the cavalry, commanded by his cousin Prince Rupert, was very effective. But the problem with Rupert's cavalry was that they charged fast and furiously and then went on to loot the enemy's supplies, leaving the rest of the army to fight the battle.

The Parliamentary General, Oliver Cromwell, realised a highly disciplined force was needed to resist these fearsome charges. Cromwell chose only the most tough and dedicated men who, after they had fought success-fully against the king, earned the nickname 'Ironsides'.

Cromwell's methods soon spread to the rest of the Parliamentary army. The 'New Model Army' was set up and organised in the same way as Cromwell's Ironsides.

Musketeer – muskets were useless if it was raining and they took about three minutes to reload.

Source A   The weapons of war

Pikeman – he is carrying an 18 foot long pike used to break up cavalry charges.

Archers were still used during the Civil War.

Source B

Members of the English Civil War Society dress in costumes of the time and recreate Civil War battles.

Source C

Soldiers were paid less than farm labourers and sometimes the commanders had no money to pay them. Many deserted or found what they could by stealing.

Source D

Many ordinary women followed the armies to look after their partners, or for adventure. This picture comes from the front of a ballad sheet which tells the story of a girl who dressed up as a soldier to go to war. She remained undiscovered until she became pregnant.

Source E   Lady Chomley's tombstone

My dear wife endured much hardship and though she is timid, like all her sex, she struggled against all the dangers and showed a courage above her sex.

Lady Chomley had led the defence of Scarborough Castle during the Royalist bombardment in 1665.

Checklist

- The Stuart kings quarrelled with their Parliaments over how to share the power to run the country.

- These quarrels became so bitter that they broke out into civil war.

- Parliament won the Civil War and the king was executed.

Activities

1. a) What were the advantages and disadvantages of the weapons used in civil war battles? (Source A)

    b) You have an army of 20 units. Each unit is made up of either archers (A), pikemen (P), musketeers (M) or cavalry (C). Choose how many units of each type of soldier you will have. Explain why you have chosen this army.

    c) Show the arrangement for battle using the capital letters. What is you army best suited for: attack or defence? Explain your answer.

2. Why do you think people join the English Civil War Society? (Source B)

3. a) Describe the soldier in Source C.

    b) Why is he pictured like this?

    c) Why might it be difficult to command armies during the Civil War?

4. What do Sources D and E tell us about attitudes to women at this time?

5 EXPERIMENTS IN GOVERNMENT

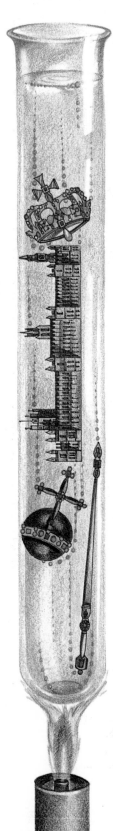

1649   Parliament abolishes the monarchy and the House of Lords.

1658   Oliver Cromwell dies.

1660   Charles I's son, Charles II, is asked by Parliament to become king.

1685   Charles II dies leaving no legitimate children. His brother James becomes king as James II. James is a Catholic.

1688   Parliament fears James will make England a Catholic country once again. He is replaced by the Dutch Protestant leader, William of Orange, who has married James's daughter Mary.

1702   William dies and is succeeded by the last Stuart to rule Britain, Anne. She is James II's youngest daughter.

1715   Anne dies. James II's son sees a chance to win back the crown. His rebellion fails. The crown goes to a different branch of the family. George of Hanover becomes King of Britain.

1745   James II's grandson Charles (Bonnie Prince Charlie) invades Scotland and England. He is defeated at the Battle of Culloden.

Themes

How shall Britain be governed? How much power should Parliament and the monarch have? Reaching an agreement on the balance of power between monarch and Parliament was difficult.

Should the monarch have all the power, share power with Parliament, or should Parliament rule without a king? Now that King Charles was dead the men in control had to decide what form of government they wanted. In practice this meant that the commander-in-chief of Parliament's army, Oliver Cromwell, would decide.

This chapter will deal with the following questions.

- What sort of government did Oliver Cromwell set up?

- Why did Parliament bring back the Stuart monarchs after the death of Cromwell?

- Why was James II, the last of the male Stuart kings, forced to leave Britain in what became known as the 'bloodless' or 'glorious' revolution of 1688?

We begin by listening to Oliver Cromwell as he thinks about the problem of governing Britain. His words are imaginary, but based on his writings and speeches.

Focus Activities

1. What sort of government does Cromwell seem to want?

2. Why did Cromwell believe that 'men of property' were the best people to run the country?

3. If the Earl of Southampton had been able to reply to Cromwell, what reasons might he have given for keeping a monarchy?

A nation ruled by God

Charles I's body lay in a coffin at St James's Palace for a week. The head had been sewn back on to the body. Only a handful of people were allowed to come and see it. Guarding the body was Charles's loyal follower, the Earl of Southampton.

Later a story was told of a mysterious, muffled visitor who entered the room at midnight and gazed in silence at the body for a long time. As he moved away from the corpse, he uttered the words, 'Cruel necessity'. No one knew who the man was. But by the voice and walk the Earl of Southampton was convinced that the midnight visitor was none other than the commander of Parliament's New Model Army, Oliver Cromwell.

What else may have run through the thoughts of General Cromwell as he stared into the coffin at Charles?

'At last it has come to this. He was given every chance to rule within the law and with the aid of Parliament. He threw these chances aside and claimed he answered to no one but God. Well, only God can answer him now.

The fault was in the man, not in the idea of kings. Too much power must lead to misuse of power. If a king cannot rule with Parliament then we must have no kings.

Nor can we trust the power of the common man. He has no understanding beyond what fills his belly. How can one trust government to a mob!

Only God-fearing men of property have the sense, provided they act according to God's wishes.'

But how was this God-fearing republic to be governed? Cromwell had to come up with some answers.

Oliver Cromwell

Charles I was dead and the monarchy and House of Lords abolished. Many people could not believe what had happened. For as long as they could remember Britain had been ruled by kings and queens.

Only tiny nations, like the Swiss and Dutch, chose not to have a monarch. Every other powerful country in Europe had a monarch. How would Britain be governed? Would there be disorder and chaos?

The execution of the king left Cromwell and his army in charge. His first step was to set up a republic. He called this republic the 'Commonwealth'. Cromwell allowed freedom of worship for everybody. The Church of England was no longer the official religion. Puritan influence was at its height during this period.

Cromwell faced quarrels amongst his own followers and rebellions by Royalists – in Ireland 1649, Scotland 1650 and England 1651. MPs argued endlessly over how people should worship and failed to pass laws to defend the country. In 1653, tired of the squabblings of Parliament, Cromwell went down to the House of Commons with a company of musketeers and turned all the members out.

Cromwell kept power in his own hands until his death in 1658. He made attempts to set up different Parliaments but none succeeded. In 1655 he divided the country into eleven districts ruled by the army. For more than a year after he died there was chaos. To end this uncertainty General George Monck marched on London and persuaded Parliament to ask Charles I's son to return to England as King Charles II.

Source A How shall Britain be governed? – The choices

Oliver Cromwell

The Republicans

They wanted an end to the monarchy but were not sure how to replace it.

'I can tell you, sirs, what government I would not have, though I cannot tell you what I would have.'

Oliver Cromwell, 1641

Most of Cromwell's supporters came from small landowners, merchants and Puritans.

The Levellers

They wanted to give every man the vote and freedom of worship. They had supporters in the army and led two unsuccessful rebellions.

'No man was born marked by God above another, therefore the poorest has a right to vote as the richest and the greatest.'

John Lilburne, one of the leaders of the Levellers. He was put in prison by Cromwell.

The Diggers

They wanted everyone in society to be equal and thought that this could only happen if everybody owned the land together. When they tried to farm common land, they were chased off by mobs hired by landowners.

'Freedom is the man who will turn the world upside down. It is no wonder that he will have enemies.'

Gerrard Winstanley, one of the leaders of the Diggers, 1650

Charles II

The Royalists

They wanted to recall Charles I's sons from exile in France and make one of them king. Most of the Royalists were larger landowners.

Source B

Cromwell will lay his hand upon his heart and call God to record that he tells the truth. He will weep, howl, say he is sorry even while he sticks a knife under your fifth rib.

Gerrard Winstanley, a Digger, 1650

Source C

In a word, Cromwell had all the wickedness for which Hell fire is ready, but also some virtues, and he will be looked upon as a brave bad man.

Earl of Clarendon, a Royalist, 1662

Source D

A huge soul, I think, have I seen only in this man. Cromwell lived and died close to God. He wanted the welfare of his people and he wanted peace.

John Maidstone, Cromwell's servant, 1658

Source E

What a gallant servant of God Cromwell once was and how many glorious and great victories God once gave him. And then said I, 'Alas, it ended like this?'

Edward Burrough, a Puritan MP, 1672

Source F   Cromwell turns out the MPs from the House of Commons in 1653

Activities

1. Read Source A. Why do you think Cromwell opposed the views of the Diggers, Levellers and Royalists? Think about who his main supporters were.

2. Compare Sources B, C, D and E.
   a) In what ways are they similar and different?
   b) Why might these writers hold these opinions of Cromwell?
   c) Can only one of these sources be true?

3. Cromwell was criticised for throwing out MPs and ruling without Parliament (Source F). Why do you think he was criticised?

The restoration of monarchy

On the 29th of May 1660, Charles II made a triumphal return to London as King of England. No one in Parliament, however, wanted to put the clock back to the reign of his father Charles I. King and Parliament must work together according to the constitution (laws) of the country.

Before Charles returned he made a promise to rule according to the laws of England (Source B). The agreement worked well until it was discovered that Charles promised to help Louis, King of France, in his war against Holland and to declare himself a Catholic. In return Louis promised him £160,000 and the help of French troops if he needed them.

Charles's action raised all the fears of a Catholic take-over. These fears came to a head in 1678 when anti-Catholic riots broke out in London. During the riots some MPs tried to get a bill passed banning Catholics from being kings and queens of England. This was known as the Exclusion Bill and was aimed at James, Charles's brother. James had declared himself openly as a Catholic.

Charles responded by dissolving Parliament and ruling without it until his death in 1685. He died having declared himself a Catholic.

It seemed the monarchy had won against the opposition in Parliament.

Source A   Oliver Cromwell's head

Fifty people were punished for the execution of Charles I and eleven executed. The body of Oliver Cromwell was dug up after the Restoration and hanged at Tyburn.

Returning Royalists got their houses and lands back unless they had been fairly sold.

Source B   The Settlement

1. The army was paid-off and disbanded.
2. Church of England restored.
3. All MPs, town councillors and clergy had to be members of the Church of England.
4. House of Lords restored.
5. Parliament controlled the king's finances.
6. Charles could choose his own advisers.
7. Charles could decide when to call Parliament.

Source C

This measure seems to be a return to the Commonwealth and not fit for a monarchy.

The Earl of Clarendon's response to the House of Commons when they asked to inspect the king's finances, 1667

Source D

This government has the appearance of being a monarchy, but at bottom it is very far from being a monarchy. The Members of Parliament are not only allowed to speak their minds freely, but also to do a number of surprising things, and even to appoint judges.

De Cominges, French Ambassador to England, 1664

Source E

Let the king come in and call a Parliament of the greatest Cavaliers and let them sit for seven years and they will become Commonwealth men.

Sir John Harrington, a Republican, 1660

Source F   The Popish Plot

Titus Oates presents his 'evidence' of a Catholic plot to kill Charles to the King's Council.

Five Catholics being hung for supposedly being involved in the Popish Plot.

Titus Oates in the stocks after he was discovered to have lied.

> There has been, and still is, a damnable and hellish plot by the Pope's agents, for the murder of the king, for overthrowing the government and rooting out and destroying the Protestant religion.
>
> *Ashley Cooper, the Earl of Shaftesbury, 1678. He led the MPs who supported the Exclusion Bill.*

> The plot must be handled as if it were true, whether it be true or not.
>
> *Charles Montague, Earl of Halifax, Charles's adviser, 1678*

Source G

> I will never yield. The older I grow, the more satisfied I become. I have reason and law on my side.
>
> *Charles's response to Ashley Cooper, the Earl of Shaftesbury, on the matter of the Exclusion Bill.*

Activities

1. Read Source A. Many people had taken part in the civil war against Charles I. Why were so few people punished?

2. Read Sources B and D. Why do you think De Cominges, the French Ambassador, made these comments?

3. How might Source C explain why the Earl of Clarendon became unpopular with Parliament?

4. What does Sir John Harrington mean when he writes that Cavaliers will become 'Commonwealth men'? (Source E)

5. Why would Titus Oates's story (Source F) be useful to those who supported the Exclusion Bill?

6. Why did the king's advisers take Titus Oates's story seriously?

7. Compare Source F with Source G. Why was Charles prepared to make a stand over the Exclusion Bill but not over the execution of Catholics during the Popish Plot?

James II and Parliament

In 1685, Charles had a fit and died, leaving the country quiet and united. But King James II, who succeeded him, was worried.

After all it had not been long since some Members of Parliament had tried to exclude James from the throne for his Catholic faith. What was more, he had set himself the difficult task of allowing everyone freedom of worship.

James's fears became a reality within his first year as king. A rebellion broke out in Dorset and Somerset led by the Protestant Duke of Monmouth. He was an illegitimate son of Charles II. Monmouth found little support. His rag-bag army of peasants was easily defeated and he was executed.

James survived his first year as king but he could not be sure of the loyalty of Parliament and the army. James needed supporters in high places. He therefore decided to appoint Catholic officers and arrange for the election of Catholic MPs.

When he tried to allow religious freedom, however, he faced stiff opposition from the Archbishop of Canterbury and the bishops. James had them tried but they were found not guilty. To many, it looked as though James was plotting a Catholic take-over.

Only one thing seemed to hold people back. James was 55 and had no sons. He could not live forever. When he died he would be succeeded by his daughter, Mary, a Protestant who had married William of Orange, the Dutch Protestant leader.

All these hopes were upset when James's second wife, Mary of Modena, gave birth to a son. Tongues began to wag. Was it really their baby? Had it been smuggled into the bedroom in the bedpan? Worse, wherever the baby came from, it was certain that it would be brought up a Catholic.

Source A   The baby in the bedpan

These pans were filled with coals and used to warm the beds. There was a story that James's 'son' was smuggled into the bedroom in a bedpan.

Source B   James II's 'son'

Mary of Modena, James II's wife, gave birth to five children between 1672-82. None survived.

There were two midwives in attendance for the birth of James's son, Mrs de Labadie and Mrs Wilkins. They both received £500 from James – an enormous sum of money at that time.

Dr Hugh Chamberlain, the royal doctor, was not at the birth as he was attending another patient several miles away. Bishop Burnet spread the story that the doctor had been deliberately sent away. Bishop Burnet was a leading Protestant in the Church of England.

Dr Chamberlain said he was angry about the story and that the queen had given birth earlier than expected.

Mrs Wilkins, the midwife, complained, 'Will they not let the infant alone? I am certain no strange child was brought in a warming pan. I was in close attendance at all times.'

Activities

1. William of Orange had sent troops to help James put down Monmouth's rebellion. Why do you think he did this?

2. Why do you think so many people were prepared to believe the story of the 'baby in the bedpan'? (Sources A and B)

The Glorious Revolution, 1688

The birth of a son to James meant another Catholic king would follow after his death. It looked as though the Protestant religion would be replaced by the Catholic faith.

A group of powerful noblemen led by the Earl of Shaftesbury decided it was time to get rid of James. They invited William of Orange, the Protestant ruler of Holland, who had married James's daughter Mary, to become King of England.

Feeling his cause was hopeless James fled to France, leaving William to enter London in triumph. The overthrow of James is known as the 'The Glorious Revolution'.

But William had no right to be king. Parliament got round this by declaring that James deserved to lose the crown because he had ignored the laws of England. Parliament did not want this to happen again, so they made William and Mary agree to certain conditions if he was to remain king.

This agreement was known as the Bill of Rights.

Source B

Coin of William and Mary's reign

Source A   Bill of Rights, 1691

1) The king must obey the laws made by Parliament.

2) The king could not have his own private army.

3) Parliament must meet frequently.

4) Judges were to be appointed by Parliament and not the king.

Later laws affecting monarch and Parliament during William and Mary's reign

1) New Parliaments had to be called every three years.

2) Money for the king had to be voted for by MPs each year.

3) Laws raising new armies had to be renewed each year.

4) Everyone but Catholics were given the freedom of worship in their chosen religion.

5) The kings and queens of England had to be Protestants.

6) MPs were to have freedom of speech.

Activities

1. The overthrow of James is known as 'The Glorious Revolution'.
   a) Which groups of people would agree with this description?
   b) Which groups would not agree with this description?

2. At first Parliament wanted Mary to be queen by herself. William replied, 'I have not come to England to be my wife's servant'. The solution is shown in Source B. What was it?

3. Historians call this agreement to share power between monarch and Parliament a 'contract'. (Source A)

   a) What is a 'contract'?
   b) Do you think this is the right word to use to describe the agreement between king and Parliament? Give reasons for your answer.

4. The end of James's reign is called a 'revolution'.

   a) What does the word 'revolution' mean?
   b) Is 'revolution' the right word to use to describe this event? Explain your answer.

5. What were the main changes in the way monarch and Parliament ruled between the time of Elizabeth and that of William and Mary?

Constitutional Monarchy

The monarch still had a great deal of power. He chose his ministers, commanded the army and navy, and could give powerful positions to people of his choice. Parliament, however, controlled the finances of the country. The monarch, therefore, could do little without its agreement.

Monarchs could no longer rule without Parliament and must obey the law like any other subject. This is known as a constitutional monarchy.

In March 1702 William died and his sister-in-law, Anne, became queen. Queen Anne was pregnant seventeen times but none of her children survived. When Anne died in 1714, the best claim to the throne of England was James II's son. Parliament did not want a Catholic ruler and so the crown passed to a distant cousin, George, the Elector of Hanover in Germany. Rebellions broke out in 1715 and 1745 to restore the Stuarts but both attempts failed.

One of the reasons for the lack of support for the Stuarts was the work done by Robert Walpole (1676-1745) who was in charge of the country for 21 years. He helped pass many laws which made England wealthy.

Walpole remained in power by leading a group of politicians who controlled Parliament from 1721-42. He also had the support of the king. He became, in effect, the leading or prime minister.

The Parliament Walpole did so much to control was very different from that of today. In the eighteenth century only a few wealthy men had the vote and they had to declare their vote at a public meeting. This meant it was easy to use bribes. Some voters were bribed as much as £100. As this made elections expensive, the government decided they would take place every seven years instead of three.

The development of Parliament, monarchy and elections was to change considerably over the next 250 years before they became the Parliamentary democracy we know today.

Source A   The Stuarts and Hanoverians

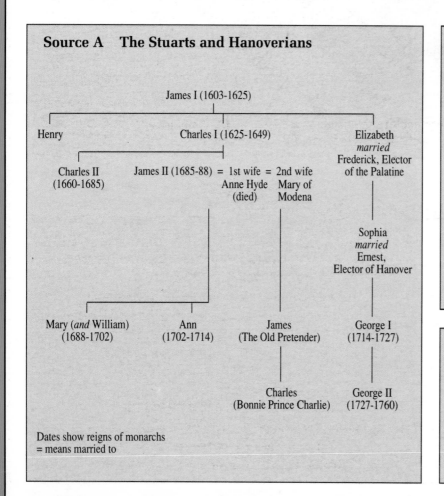

Dates show reigns of monarchs
= means married to

James I (1603-1625)

Henry — Charles I (1625-1649) — Elizabeth *married* Frederick, Elector of the Palatine

Charles II (1660-1685)   James II (1685-88) = 1st wife Anne Hyde (died) = 2nd wife Mary of Modena

Sophia *married* Ernest, Elector of Hanover

Mary (*and* William) (1688-1702)   Ann (1702-1714)   James (The Old Pretender)   George I (1714-1727)

Charles (Bonnie Prince Charlie)   George II (1727-1760)

Source B   Sir Robert Walpole

'Every man has his price.'

Sir Robert Walpole's saying

Source C

Robert Walpole's policy was simple – avoiding war, encouraging trade, reducing taxes. As he rightly said, 'I am no saint, no reformer'.

J H Plumb, 'England in the 18th Century', 1950

Source D   Sir Robert Walpole

First Lord of the Treasury, Mr Walpole, Chancellor of the Exchequer Mr Walpole, Clerk of the Courts Mr Walpole's son. In charge of Customs duties of London, Mr Walpole's second son. Secretary of the Treasury, Mr Walpole's brother. Postmaster General, Mr Walpole's brother. Secretary to Ireland, Mr Walpole's brother. Secretary to the Postmaster General, Mr Walpole's brother-in-law.

From a London newspaper, 1732

Source E   An 18th century election – a painting by William Hogarth

Voters had to mount the platform and openly declare their vote. This meant they could be bribed. The voters on the stairs include the sick, the mentally ill, a dying man and a prisoner in leg irons.

Activities

1. Look at Source A.
   a) Who should have been the rightful ruler after the death of Anne?
   b) Why was he not chosen as the next monarch?

2. Read Sources B, C and D.
   How do they help to explain why Robert Walpole stayed in power for so long?

3. What do you think William Hogarth is trying to tell us about elections in the 18th century? (Source E)

Checklist

- Between 1649-1660 England was a republic ruled by Oliver Cromwell.

- The monarchy was restored in 1660 but Parliament placed a number of restrictions on royal power.

- James II was suspected of wanting to overthrow the Protestant Church. He was forced to leave England in what became known as 'The Glorious Revolution'.

- Britain became a constitutional monarchy but there were still many differences compared to today's political system.

Scotland	England and Wales	Ireland

1536 — Henry VIII's Parliament passes an Act which divides Wales into counties with the same system of law as England. Wales sends MPs to Parliament in London.

1587 — Execution of Mary, Queen of Scots.

1599 — Rebellion in Ireland.

1599 -1603 — English conquest of Ireland.

1603 — James VI of Scotland becomes King James I of England.

1640 — Scotland invades England.

1642 — Outbreak of civil war in England.

1649 — Rebellion in Ireland put down savagely by Oliver Cromwell. Scottish Protestants are given land in Northern Ireland to settle. Laws are passed reducing the power of Irish Catholics.

1689 — Rebellion in Ireland led by King James II.

1707 — Union of England and Scotland. The Scottish Parliament is closed down. Scottish MPs attend Parliament in London.

1715 — Rebellion in Scotland by James II's son, also called James.

1745 — Rebellion in Scotland led by James II's grandson Charles (Bonnie Prince Charlie).

Themes

The United Kingdom today is made up of four countries: England, Wales, Scotland and Northern Ireland. Before the time of the Tudor monarchs these were all independent countries apart from Wales. Wales had been conquered by England in the 13th century.

Scotland, on the other hand, had defeated the English at the Battle of Bannockburn (1314) and had kept its independence, with its own monarch.

The English attempted to hold on to Ireland but their efforts met with little success. By the time of the Tudors, they had only managed to keep a toe-hold in Ireland in the area surrounding Dublin, known as the 'Pale'.

By 1750 the situation was very different. Scotland, Ireland and Wales were under the political control of England.

This chapter looks at the following questions.

- Why did England seek control of Scotland, Ireland and Wales?

- How did she achieve this control, and how successful was it?

The Focus looks at the dangerous state of the border between England and Scotland during the 16th century. This letter was sent to Sir Richard Carey, the March Warden (he controlled law and order on the border) from his deputy, Henry Widdrington.

Focus Activities

1. From the English point of view make a list of the crimes committed by the Armstrongs.

2. What does the letter tell us about the amount of control that English and Scottish governments had over the border country?

3. Henry Widdrington was very worried when he sent this letter to the March Warden. Can you suggest why?

4. What reasons might stop the English sending a large army to destroy the Armstrongs?

Border troubles

The people of the Marches

To Sir Richard Carey, Warden of the English Middle March, May 18, 1599

Your Lordship,

In my last letter I wrote to you what I knew of Mr Rydley's death. Since then I have learned more details.

It appears Mr Rydley discovered that six of the Armstrongs were to cross the border. They were going to play the Bewcastle men at football and follow this with a session of hard drinking.

He decided that this was the ideal time to catch these great Scottish thieves and murderers. Together with the captain of Bewcastle he planned a trap. They assembled a body of over 50 men and lay in wait.

The Armstrongs, however, found out about the ambush and came in force – over 200 of them. They took Mr Rydley's group by surprise. The results were grim.

Over 30 prisoners and 50 horses were taken back across the border and are now up for ransom. Mr Rydley and Mr Welton had their throats cut, whilst John Whytfield was slashed across the stomach and his bowels spilled out. He has been sewed up and though he is still alive we expect news of his death at any time.

The Armstrongs were seen as troublemakers by both Scottish and English monarchs. This painting shows Johnny Armstrong with his men leaving their stronghold to meet King James V of Scotland. When they arrived James had them all hung.

Your Lordship commanded me to call out all the armed men of the district to pursue the Armstrongs, but I regret I cannot do this. The countryside is in turmoil. The local men dare not take action while they know their friends are held prisoner.

I hope your Lordship will make known the work of Thomas Musgrave in this affair. His son-in-law, living in his house with him, is the murderer of Mr Rydley. No doubt when Her Majesty hears of this outrage it will please her to make you the instrument of her revenge.

I have better news, however, from our part of the border. The outlaws have never rested since you left, even daring to rob within a mile of the city walls of Newcastle. However with my own men I have hunted and killed Thomas Rotherforth and Nychol Hall.

Henry Widdrington, Deputy Warden

England's fears

Everyone needs good neighbours. But supposing your neighbours are like the Armstrongs in the Focus. How can you hit back if they can find safety over the border? If you take an army to chase them then you are guilty of invading a foreign country and that means war.

England was the most powerful nation in the British Isles. Nevertheless she feared that her neighbours' countries could be used to shelter her enemies and as a base for invasion.

It was this fear, and the desire for greater wealth, that led England to seek political control over her neighbours.

Activities

1. Look at the map below.
    What were the possible threats to England from the following countries?

    a) Wales

    b) Scotland

    c) Ireland

England and her neighbours in the early Tudor period

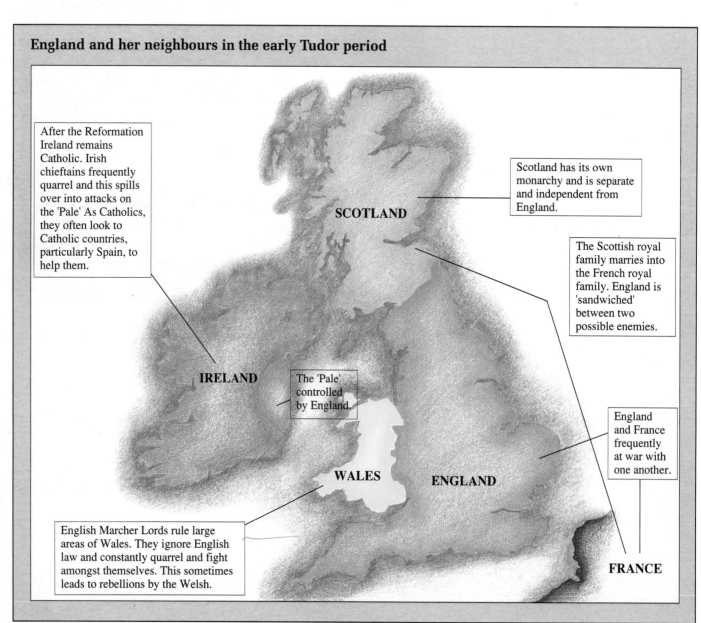

After the Reformation Ireland remains Catholic. Irish chieftains frequently quarrel and this spills over into attacks on the 'Pale' As Catholics, they often look to Catholic countries, particularly Spain, to help them.

Scotland has its own monarchy and is separate and independent from England.

The Scottish royal family marries into the French royal family. England is 'sandwiched' between two possible enemies.

SCOTLAND

IRELAND

The 'Pale' controlled by England.

England and France frequently at war with one another.

WALES

ENGLAND

English Marcher Lords rule large areas of Wales. They ignore English law and constantly quarrel and fight amongst themselves. This sometimes leads to rebellions by the Welsh.

FRANCE

Wales

Wales at this time was split up into two parts. The principality of Wales had been conquered by Edward I and turned into shire counties like England. But the rest of Wales consisted of Marcher Lordships. These were lands given by William the Conqueror to powerful lords in order to hold back the Welsh. Over the years the Marcher Lords extended their control. They acted like princes, with their own law courts and private armies.

The native Welsh spoke their own language and had strong loyalties to their country but were politically weak. Indeed, after they had rebelled against King Henry IV they had their rights under the law completely removed.

The problem for the English was not so much the Welsh but the Marcher Lords. If Wales were not firmly under English control, it could be used as a base by foreign invaders. After all this is where Henry VII, the first Tudor monarch, had landed in his bid to become king.

Source A

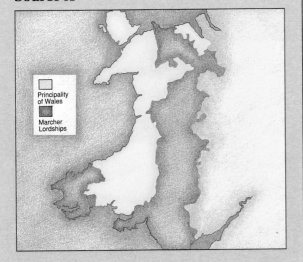

Principality of Wales

Marcher Lordships

Source B

We hear of heiresses being carried off and forcibly married, of Marcher juries refusing to find guilty obvious criminals, of witnesses disappearing from fear.

From a letter written by Rowland Lee, Bishop of Coventry, to Thomas Cromwell, Henry VIII's chief adviser, 1534. Cromwell had put Rowland Lee in charge of the Council of Wales with instructions to be very strict.

Source C

Rowland Lee was an extremely severe punisher of offenders and is said to have hanged in all 5000 evildoers.

'England and Wales under the Tudors', Sinclair Atkins, 1961

Source D

Whether Rowland Lee hanged 5000 criminals may be doubted, but he certainly established the authority of the law.

J. D. Makie, 'The Earlier Tudors', 1958

Activities

Source E   Act of Union of England and Wales 1536

1. All Wales divided into shires with English law courts. Marcher Lordships abolished.
2. Wales to send MPs to Parliament at Westminster.
3. Welshmen were to become Justices of the Peace.
4. English law extended to all of Wales.

1. Why were there Marcher Lordships on the Welsh border? (Source A)

2. What problems faced Rowland Lee? (Source B)

3. a) What is the difference in interpretation between Sources C and D?

   b) Why might Rowland Lee's reputation have been exaggerated?

4. What might the advantages and disadvantages of the Act of Union be to Welsh people?

Scotland

In 1485 Scotland was a separate, independent country. English attempts to conquer Scotland ended with the Scottish victory at Bannockburn in 1314. The Treaty of Northampton in 1328 recognised Scotland's independence.

England did not try to conquer Scotland again. However, relations between the two countries were not good. Scotland made treaties of friendship with France, England's traditional enemy. Members of the Scottish and French royal families married and French influence at the Scottish court was strong.

Whenever the Scots seemed to threaten England an army was sent north to punish them. During Henry VIII's reign there were two invasions of Scotland. Henry was at war with France and feared that the Scots would join the French.

Source D

I rejoice at the mischief, robbery and stealing which is everywhere in Scotland and I pray to God that it may continue.

Remarks made by an English visitor to Scotland after the Battle of Flodden

Source E

Put all to fire and sword, burn Edinburgh town when you have sacked and gotten what you can from it, so that it may remain forever a memory of the vengeance of God.

Instructions to the English invasion force sent to punish the Scots after they had turned down a marriage alliance between Mary, Queen of Scots, and Henry VIII's son Edward, 1544

Source A   Treaty of Perpetual Peace

A good, real, sincere, true, entirely firm peace, bond, league and alliance on land and sea, to last forever.

Peace treaty signed by James IV of Scotland and Henry VII of England, 1502

Source B

I am the owner of Scotland which you hold only by doing homage to me.

Henry VIII's reply to James IV of Scotland, 1513. James had asked Henry to make peace with France.

Source C   Battle of Flodden

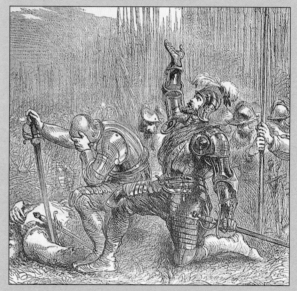

In August 1513, while Henry VIII was invading France, James IV of Scotland invaded England. The Scots were defeated at Flodden and James killed. This picture shows prayers before the battle.

Activities

1. Look at Sources A and C. What happened to the Treaty of Perpetual Peace?

2. Read Source B. What do you think James IV felt about Henry's reply? Give reasons for your answer.

3. What does Source D suggest about English attitudes to the Scots?

4. Read Source E. Why was Henry so annoyed when the Scots turned down the marriage of his son to Mary?

In 1603, on the death of Elizabeth I, James VI of Scotland became James I of England. Each country remained independent with its own Parliament. It appeared that the longstanding dispute between them was now over. But although they continued to share the same monarch, relations between England and Scotland were not good.

Things came to a head in the early 1700s. The English feared that the Scottish Parliament would choose James II's son, James, a Catholic, as their next king rather than George of Hanover, England's choice. From 1701-1713 England was at war with France. There were fears that James, who was staying at the French court, would land in Scotland with a French army to claim the Scottish throne.

There seemed to be only two choices – either complete separation of England and Scotland or union. In 1707 the Act of Union was passed uniting the two countries. The Scottish Parliament was closed down and 45 Scottish MPs sent to Parliament at Westminster.

Source H

A Scotsman having problems with a toilet in London (printed in 1745)

Source F

Aliens Act 1705
Scots would be treated as aliens (foreigners) and trade with Scotland would be prohibited unless the Scots accepted George as their future king or began negotiations for union with England.

Act of Union 1707
Scotland was given complete freedom to trade with England and English colonies overseas. Nearly £400,000 was given to Scotland with which to pay off her debts.

Source G

I am old and have long experience of hard and laborious work and now of poverty. I wish to leave the nation free of the first and at least on the road to leave the other.

A Scottish government minister, c.1707

Source I   Reactions to the Act of Union

We are bought and sold for English gold.
A Scottish popular song

I never saw a nation so wild at this Union.
Daniel Defoe, an English agent in Scotland, 1709

Have we not bought the Scots, and a right to tax them? Scotland is now but a county of England.
English Member of Parliament, 1708

5. Why did Scottish MPs vote for the Act of Union? (Sources F and G)

6. Many Scots hated the union. What evidence does Source I provide for this?

7. What do Source H and the statement by the MP in Source I suggest about English attitudes towards the Scots.

The Jacobite Rebellions

James II, the Stuart King of England, Scotland and Ireland, had fled to France in 1688 (see page 45). His followers were known as Jacobites. The word comes from the Latin 'Jacobus' meaning 'James'.

In Scotland and the north of England there were people dissatisfied with the Act of Union and the choice of a German king as ruler of Britain. In 1715 a group of powerful nobles declared James II's son as James III, King of Scotland. Sadly for his followers, the new 'king' was not an enthusiastic leader and by the time he arrived in Scotland the rebellion was all but over. Five weeks later he was on his way back to France.

Thirty years went by and it looked as though the Stuarts' hopes were fading. But in 1745 Charles Edward Stuart, James III's son, landed at Moidart in the western highlands with only seven followers. Gathering an army of 5000 highlanders he crossed the border into England. Few Englishmen joined him. At Derby the highland clan chiefs told Charles they would go no further. They now began their long retreat to Scotland.

Pursued by powerful British armies the clansmen were massacred at Culloden, near Inverness. Scotland paid the price for Charles's failure. Followers of the Stuarts were rounded up and killed or transported (sent to the colonies and made to work like slaves). The wearing of the tartan was banned and the highlanders disarmed.

Was Charles interested in Scotland or was he simply using it as a stepping stone to the English crown? Whatever the answer, the Jacobite cause was finished. From then on Scotland was a part of northern Britain.

Source A

James Francis Edward Stuart – James III

Source B

To the chiefs it seemed sensible that Charles should end the Union and rule on behalf of his father in Scotland. But Charles had promised his father to win three crowns for him and so persuaded the chiefs to invade England.

Fitzroy McLean, 'Bonnie Prince Charlie', 1989

Source C

Many Scots thought that the Act of Union betrayed Scotland. While there was a Scottish Parliament few highland clan chiefs had shown any respect for it. But a Scottish king seemed to them to make more sense than a German one.

John Prebble, 'Culloden', 1961

Source D

No sir, I never thought about it. I just thought how nice it would be to plunder London.

A reply made to Lord Cockburn (1746) when he asked a highlander if he wanted to dethrone King George II.

Source E

The Jacobites were made into heroes, not so much because the Scots really wanted the Stuarts back but because they hated the English.

Janet Glover, 'The History of Scotland', 1978

Source G   The 1745 Rebellion

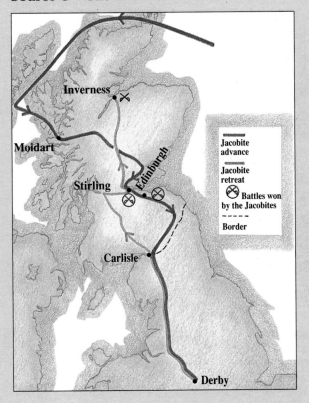

Source F

Charles Edward Stuart – 'Bonnie Prince Charlie' – in full highland dress

Activities

1. Which of the following statements do you think are true? Give reasons for your answer. Use Sources B, C, D and E.

    The Scots supported the Stuarts because:

    (i)   they thought them to be the true kings of England

    (ii) they thought them to be the true kings of Scotland

    (iii) they hated the Act of Union.

2. Why do you think Charles went no further than Derby? (Source G)

3. Draw a poster supporting the Stuarts and Scottish independence.

4. a) Why did the Scots make the Stuarts into heroes and see them as romantic and glamorous figures? (Source E)

    b) Judging by their portraits, did the Stuarts live up to this image? (Sources A and F)

Ireland – the Tudors

England had always feared that Ireland might be used as a base by her enemies. Both Spain and France had supported Irish rebellions. All the attempts by England to conquer Ireland had failed. By 1485, although Henry VII claimed to be King of all Ireland, he only controlled the area around Dublin known as the 'Pale'.

The Reformation made relations between the two countries even worse. England became Protestant, Ireland remained Catholic. To prevent any challenge to his rule, Henry VIII declared himself Head of the Church in Ireland.

Thereafter the English attempted several ways to subdue the Irish. Firstly, through force and terror. Secondly, from the time of Mary Tudor onwards, by driving the native Irish off their land and replacing them with loyal Protestant English and Scottish settlers. Whatever method the English tried, it proved very expensive. In most years it cost more to rule Ireland than was gained through trade with Ireland.

Source A

We drove the Irish from the plains into the woods, where they would freeze or die of hunger with the onset of winter. How godly it is to overthrow so wicked a race. To my thoughts this is the greatest sacrifice we can offer to God. We did kill women and children and even those that did not fight so that we could kill the men of war by famine.

The heads of the killed were cut from their bodies and lined the route to the tents. All who entered passed the heads and this did bring great terror to them when they saw the heads of their dead fathers, brothers, children and friends.

Thomas Churchyard, who accompanied an English military expedition to Ulster, 1574

Source B

It was not too long ago, the Irish lived as barbarians, in woods, in bogs and lonely places, without law and government, neither knowing religion or even superstitious papism (Catholic religion). They steal, they are cruel and bloody, full of revenge, enjoy horrible executions, they are common rapists and murderers of children.

Barnaby Rich (an English historian), 'A New Description of Ireland', 1610

Source C

I do not think they (English scholars) should be called historians as they act like dung beetles when writing about the Irish. For it is in the behaviour of that beetle not to stop at any flower or blossom in the garden. It keeps bustling about until it meets with the dung of a horse and a cow, and then rolls around in it.

Seathrun Ceilinn (an Irish historian), 1612

Source D   John Derrick 'Image of Ireland', 1581

Source E   John Derrick 'Image of Ireland', 1581

A   Here creepes out of Sainct Filchers denne, a packe of
prowling mates,
Most hurtfull to the English pale, and noysome to the states:
Which spare no more their country byrth, then those of
th' english race,
But yeld to each a lyke good turne, when as they come in place.

B   They spoyle, and burne, and beare away, as fitte occasions
serve,
And thinke the greater ill they doe, the greater prayse deserve:

They passe not for the poore mans cry, nor yet respect his
teares,
But rather joy to see the fire, to flash about his ears.
To see both flame, and smouldring smoke, to duske the
christall skyes,
Next to their pray, therein I say, their second glory lyes.

C   And thus bereaving him of house, of cattle and of store:
They do returne backe to the wood, from whence they came
before.

Activities

1. According to Source A, how did the
English attempt to control the Irish?

2. Read Source B.

a) Do you think the English historian gives
an accurate picture of the Irish? Explain
your answer.

b) If the English believed this description,
how might it help to explain their
behaviour as outlined in Source A?

3. Read Source C.

a) How does the writer explain the view of
the Irish given by English historians?

b) Why might English historians have
been biased when writing about
Ireland?

4. Look at Sources D and E.

a) What view of the Irish is given by these
pictures?

b) What impression of the Irish do you get
from reading the verse? (Source E)

5. a) Draw a sketch of the English behaviour
described in Source A.

b) Write a verse attacking the English for
what they have done.

Ireland in the 17th century

The 17th century was to see the almost complete takeover of Irish land by England and Scottish settlers. All of County Derry was handed over to a group of London companies, while the eastern counties were settled by many thousands of Scottish Protestants.

In 1641 the Irish Catholics in Ulster rose against England hoping to win their lands back. The leaders claimed they were acting in support of King Charles I in his struggle against Parliament. There were terrible cruelties on both sides. At first the rebels were successful but in 1649 Oliver Cromwell arrived in Ireland and savagely crushed the rebellion.

After 1660, Irish fortunes improved under the restored Stuart monarchy but when many Irish Catholics rose in support of the exiled King James II they were defeated in 1690. Power now lay in the hands of Protestant landowners loyal to England. Catholics held only 20% of the land and lived in great poverty.

Their situation was made worse by a series of anti-Catholic laws. Catholics were not allowed to vote or to have jobs in government. It was forbidden to hold Catholic services or open Catholic schools. Catholics were not allowed to own land, to wear a sword (the mark of a gentleman), or to speak the Gaelic language.

Source A

This illustration comes from an anti-Catholic pamphlet published in London in 1642. It shows Irish Catholics massacring Protestants during the 1641 rebellion.

Source C

A 17th century painting showing the defeat of James II by William of Orange (King William III) at the Battle of the Boyne, 1690

Source B

It hath pleased God to bless us. The enemy were about 3000 strong in the town. I do not think 30 of the whole number escaped with their lives. Those that did will be sent to the West Indies as slaves.

I am of the opinion that this is the righteous judgement of God upon those barbarous wretches who have so much innocent blood on their hands. It will prevent the shedding of blood in the future.

Oliver Cromwell in a report to Parliament after he attacked and destroyed the town of Drogheda in 1649

Source D

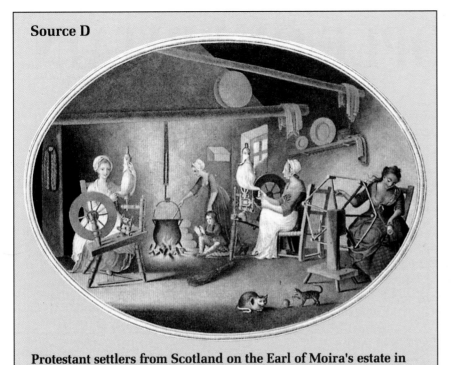

Protestant settlers from Scotland on the Earl of Moira's estate in County Down. They built up a successful linen industry.

Source E

One third of all our rents in Ireland goes to England. Add all other trade and about one half of all the wealth goes to England. The rise of rents is squeezed out of the very blood, clothes and houses of the people, who live worse than English beggars.

Jonathan Swift, 'A Short View of the State of Ireland', 1727

Source F

I have been told that a young healthy child at a year old is a most delicious, nourishing food, whether stewed, roasted, baked or boiled. I accept that this food is expensive and probably best for the landowners as they have already eaten most of the parents.

Jonathan Swift, 'A Modest Proposal', 1729

Activities

1. How can you tell the picture in Source A is anti-Catholic?

2. Look at Sources A and B.

   How could Oliver Cromwell justify the killing of men, women and children at Drogheda in 1649?

3. How do you think Irish Catholics would have felt about the people pictured in Source D? Give reasons for your answer.

4. Read Source E. Whose side do you think Jonathan Swift is on? Explain your answer.

5. Read Source F.

   a) Is Jonathan Swift serious about children being eaten?

   b) Why does he write like this?

6. In Protestant areas of Northern Ireland today there are wall paintings showing William of Orange at the Battle of the Boyne (Source C). Why do you think this is?

Checklist

- England wanted to control her neighbours – Scotland, Wales and Ireland.

- Wales was absorbed peacefully in 1536.

- In 1603 Scotland and England were ruled by the same king. They were united by the Act of Union in 1707. This Act was unpopular with many Scots.

- Ireland was forcibly taken over and settled by large numbers of English and Scottish Protestants.

Haymaking, early 17th century

Harvesting crops in India

A baby in India suffering from malnutrition

As in many Third World countries today, most people in Britain lived by farming. The most important time of the year was the harvest. A bad harvest could mean malnutrition or starvation.

Themes

Between 1500 and 1750 the population of Britain rose from around 4.5 million to about 7 million people. The medieval farming landscape of open fields was changing. They were gradually being replaced by smaller enclosed fields which were more efficient for growing food and rearing animals. At the same time huge areas of woodland were being cleared and marshes drained. For most people changes such as these were far more important than politics or religion. They directly affected their everyday lives and their ability to look after their families.

This chapter looks at the following questions.

- How was the countryside changing? What effect did this have on everyday life?

- Why were towns growing in importance?

- How was British society divided between rich and poor?

- What was family life like? What part did women play in the family?

We begin with something that was vital to the lives of everyone in early modern Britain – the weather. Late frost in the spring, too much rain or too little sun in the summer could ruin the harvest. Bad weather meant lean times, hunger, and for the poor the risk of malnutrition or starvation.

Focus Activities

1. Draw a table with two columns. Give it the same title as the Focus. In the first column write the date and kind of weather. In the second column write the effect of the weather on the crops.

2. What other problems are affecting Ralph and his community?

3. Ralph was the local vicar. What might he have said to the people in church in early July 1648?

The Lord goes against us

Death strikes an old woman.

From the diary of Ralph Josselin, Vicar of Earls Colne, Essex

September 15, 1646. A marvellous wet season, winter coming early. Wheat this year was poor and drooping. All manner of meats are very dear. Beef is the cheapest, 2½d per pound.

October 24, 1646. A wonderful sad wet season. The corn has rotted in the fields. The grass had been trodden underfoot by the cattle. There is no work. Little corn has been sown. Fears of utter ruin in the Kingdom.

August 15, 1647. Times of great sickness and illness, agues (a fever like malaria) common. Whether it arises from infected air I know not, but fruit rots on the trees and many cattle die of the murrain (foot and mouth disease). This is a warning.

September 26, 1647. The Lord hath sent a good season. Prices are very high at a rate never seen before: beef 3d, butter 6½d, cheese 4d, sugar 18d. The soldiers are returning to be housed and fed by us again.

May 9, 1648. God has punished the nation once more this spring. At the end of April, terrible frosts killed the rye. Young ashes in leaf were nipped and blackened and those shoots died.

June 28, 1648. The Lord goes against us this season. Much was carried away with the floods. The corn is pulled down by weeds.

Death snatches a young child from a poor family.

Town and country

Most British people spent their lives in the countryside – in farmsteads, hamlets and villages. It was here that the greatest achievement of the age gradually took place – producing enough food to meet the needs of a steadily growing population.

The demand for more food led to changes in farming. New land was brought under cultivation – marshes were drained and forests cleared. The most important change was enclosure. The large open fields and commons of the Middle Ages were broken up and enclosed. New smaller fields were fenced off so they could be farmed more efficiently.

Sometimes enclosure was done by force – by the landowner, sometimes by agreement between the villagers. Often the first areas to be enclosed were the wastelands, woods and commons around a village.

In general enclosure led to increased food production and bigger profits for many farmers. However this had a cost. Life became even harder for poor families who had depended on using common grazing and woodlands. Some were driven off the land altogether.

Source A

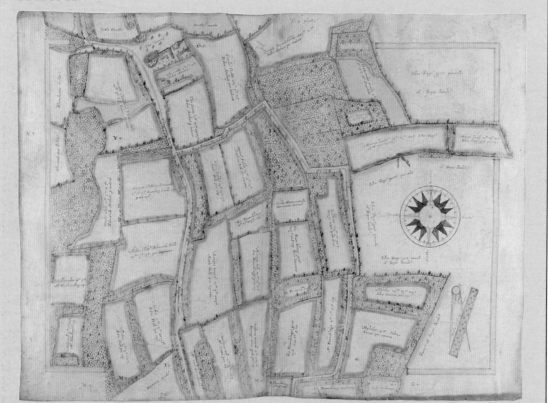

A map of Edgeware, Middlesex in 1597. It shows a forest area being cleared to make small fields.

Source B

John Spencer changed lands from growing crops into pasture for sheep and other animals. This meant four persons were made beggars who up till then had been living and working there.

A government report in 1517. Spencer was a large landowner, one of many who could make more money from keeping sheep for wool than from the rents payed by poor farmers.

Source C

At Woodthorpe, in Leicestershire, the villagers agreed to enclose their lands in 1663 because of the many squabbles amongst them. Their arable (land for crops), meadow, pasture and grass lands were so mixed up that they reported, 'great waste and spoil hath been done in their corn and grassland'.

Michael Reed, 'The Age of Exuberance 1550-1700', 1986

In 1500 most towns were very small, often no bigger than a handful of streets. For example, Liverpool, Manchester and Birmingham were little more than villages. However by 1750 one person in five lived in a town. This had a dramatic effect on the economy of the country. Townspeople make goods and provide services which can be sold. This might be to the farms and villages around them, to other parts of the country, or overseas. Gradually towns became the main centres of wealth and power in Britain.

Source D   Newcastle

NEWE:CASTLE

A	Kings maner
B	Kings Lodgings
C	Grammer Schole
D	The manner
F	Newe house
H	Black friers
I	Saint Johns
K	High Castle
L	Almose Houses
M	Saint Nicholas
N	Alhallowes
O	Trinitie House
P	Pandon Hall
Q	The wall Knoll
R	The Stone Hill
S	The maisen deeu
T	Almose Houses
V	West Spittle
W	White Friers
X	Scottish Inne
Z	Newe yate
3	West gate
4	Pandon yate
6	Sandgate yate
7	Close gate
8	The Key.

A Scale of Paſes.
30   100   150   200

Deſcribed by
William Matthew.

This map was drawn in 1610. Newcastle was an important trading city.

Activities

1. How can we tell from Source A that the fields have been cleared from a large woodland area?

2. What would the poor of a village lose if the local woods and commons were enclosed by a landlord.

3. There were landlords like John Spencer in Source B all over the country. How might their actions have encouraged the growth of towns and trade. Use Source E in your answer.

4. Why were the villagers in Source C happy to agree to enclose their land?

5. Look at Source E. Why were towns so important when most people lived in the countryside?

6. Look at Source D. In what ways is Newcastle in 1610 still a medieval city?

7. Look at the scale on Source D. Using your own pace as a guide, work out the circumference of the city walls.

Source E

Sandhill is a market for fish and other goods. It is easily used by merchants and all those that live by shipping. There is a long quay where ships lie safe from storms.

The flesh (meat) market is I think the greatest in England. The reason is not the size of the town. It is the people within ten miles who do their buying there. Also all that live by the coal trade and the shipping which comes into the river for coal, sometimes 300 ships.

A survey of Newcastle-upon-Tyne in 1649

63

Rich and poor

When British people met one another their first thought might well be, 'What is this person's rank?' By this they meant is this person more or less important than me? The answer was usually easy to see. Clothes, and manners set people apart. They were clues to their type of family and wealth.

British society was deeply divided. A walk down the street of any town showed enormous differences in standards of living, from great landowners to beggars. The way people behaved towards one another depended on the rank or social class they were born into.

Many families struggled to survive. Between 20% and 30% of the population lived on the edge of starvation. By 1601 this problem was so great that the government brought in the Poor Law. This ordered every parish to look after its own poor and pay for this by collecting a tax on property.

Source A

We in England divide our people into four sorts, gentlemen, citizens or burgesses (townspeople), yeomen (farmers) and labourers (farm workers).

William Harrison, a clergyman writing in 1577

Source B

Type of households	Numbers of households	Average size of household	Numbers of persons	Numbers of children	Numbers of servants
Gentry	3	9.0	27	7	15
Yeomen	26	5.8	151	64	34
Tradesmen	9	3.9	35	16	2
Labourers	12	3.2	38	15	0
Poor Men	12	2.1	25	11	0
Totals	62	4.45	276	113	51

This table shows the five types of people in the parish of Goodnestone-next-Wingham in Kent. It is based on a survey conducted by the curate in 1676.

Source C

The glaring fact is that the life of the labourer was a constant battle for survival. Labouring families lived in poor one room cottages, with little furniture and on a diet of bread, cheese, lard, soup, weak beer and garden greens.

Keith Wrightson, 'English Society 1580-1680', 1982

Source E

By 1572 further laws were needed since all parts of the kingdom were 'presently with rogues, vagabonds and sturdy beggars exceedingly pestered, by means whereof horrible murders, thefts and other great outrages happen daily'. In that year vagabonds who could not give a satisfactory account of themselves and were over fourteen were to be whipped and burned through the gristle of the right ear.

Christopher Hibbert, 'The English 1066-1945', 1987

Source D

A wealthy man passes a beggar on a country road.

Source F

1697: Paid for washing Edward Sare, 6d. For a shirt for him 2s 0½d. For Linsey Wolsey to make him clothes, 8d. For mending his shoes 1s 2d.

1698: Paid for ale and bread for Edward Sare, 8d. For a powder for his mouth 4d. For cloth for britches, 3s 0d. For oatmeal 7d.

An extract from the Poor Law accounts for the parish of Ripley in Derbyshire.

Source G

In London the rich look down on the poor. The courtier the townsman. The townsman the countryman. The merchant the retailer. The shopkeeper the craftsman. The better sort of craftsman the poorer. The shoemaker the cobbler. The cobbler the cartman.

Thomas Nash, 1593. Nash was a satirist. This meant he wrote sharply and amusingly about the way people behaved.

Source H

This painting shows the squire of the village of Tichbourne in Hampshire giving out food to the poor in 1670. This was done with great ceremony every year.

Activities

1. What is the same and what is different about the way Sources A and B divide people into types? Can you suggest reasons for the differences?

2. In Source B what percentage of the villagers were poor?

3. Think about the Focus in this chapter. What effect might a bad harvest have on the labourers and the poor? (Sources B and C)

4. What might the men in Source D be saying to each other?

5. What does Source F indicate about the treatment of the poor in Ripley? Why is this treatment different from Source E?

6. What point is Nash trying to make in Source G?

7. Is the squire in Source H just being kind to the poor, or might he have something to gain from this ceremony?

Women and family

The family was the basic building block for society in early modern Britain. Usually this would be the kind of family most common today, two parents and their children. Living with them, however, there was often a wider household which might include other relatives, servants and apprentices. For many the family also gave them a job. Most craftsmen and farmers worked from their homes with their wives and children as their main workforce.

Family life varied according to how rich people were but in all classes the husband was in charge. Women were seen as inferior to men and expected to do as they were told. Despite this, however, many wives were treated as equals by their husbands.

Source A

From the 16th century the parish registers recorded the baptisms, marriages and burials of the people of thousands of villages and towns. After studying this evidence we can state with some confidence that around 1600 the average lifespan of English villagers was about 38 years; that something like a fifth of all children born died in the first year of life; that a quarter to a third died before the age of 10; that of those who grew up most would die before 60. Marriages were broken by death as commonly as they are by divorce today.

Keith Wrightson, 'Love, Marriage and Death', 1986

Source C

The husband is the highest in the family, and has authority over all in his care; he is as a king in his own house. But if love be not the guiding hand in the husband there is likely to be little peace between man and wife.

Christopher Hibbert, 'The English 1066-1945', 1987

Source B   A farmer's wife

It is a wife's occupation to winnow all manner of corn, to make malt, wash and wring, to make hay, shear corn and in time of need to help her husband to fill the dung cart, drive the plough, to load hay and such other, to go to market to sell butter, cheese, milk, eggs, chickens, capons, hens, pigs, geese and all manner of corn.

Anthony Fitzherbert, 'The Boke of Husbandrie', 1523. This extract lists the jobs expected of a farmer's wife.

Source D

A husband beating his wife

Source E

Now the women folk of England are fair and pretty. They have far more freedom than in other lands and know just how to make good use of it. They often stroll out or drive out by coach in very gorgeous clothes and the men must put up with such ways and may not punish them for it. Indeed the good wives often beat their men.

Thomas Platter, 'Travels in England', 1599

Source F

This picture shows a mother in a wealthy family being cared for just after the birth of her baby.

Source G

The tomb of Lady Margaret Leigh and her baby at All Saints Church, Fulham. Both died in childbirth – a dangerous time because of the risk of infection.

Checklist

- Most people lived in the countryside, though growing numbers lived in towns.

- Farming was changing. More land was enclosed and food production increased.

- Society was divided into classes or ranks with a wide gap between rich and poor.

- Family life for most women consisted of hard work and the dangers of childbearing.

Activities

1. Read Source A. What were the chances of (i) living beyond the age of one, (ii) living beyond the age of ten? Give your answers as a percentage.

2. Think about Sources C and D. Do they agree on the way a husband should behave towards his family? What do they tell us about the position of women in society at the time?

3. What might a wife who has just finished the jobs mentioned in Source B say to a husband who was about to beat her?

4. In what ways does Source E disagree with Sources C and D?

5. What risks of infection are mother and child running in Source F? If you were able to offer advice what would you say?

6. How might historians use Source G?

7. What are the similarities and differences between the roles of women today and in early modern Britain?

8 SCIENCE AND THE SUPERNATURAL

1542   Witchcraft and sorcery made punishable by death.

1543   Copernicus published *De Revolutionibus* and proves the earth goes round the sun.

1604   King James I commanded that the laws against witchcraft be made harsher.

1610   Galileo discovered the moons of Jupiter.

1628   William Harvey published his discovery of the circulation of blood.

1645-7 Matthew Hopkins, the Witchfinder General, (a government witch hunter), led the trials of over 200 witches in Essex.

1662   The Royal Society is formed as a centre for scientific experiment and enquiry.

1682   The last execution for witchcraft in England.

1763   Laws against witchcraft abolished.

A MOST Certain, Strange, and true Discovery of a

VVITCH.

Being taken by some of the Parliament Forces, as she was standing on a small planck-board and sayling on it over the River of *Newbury*:

Together with the strange and true manner of her death, with the propheticall words and speeches she vsed at the same time.

Printed by John Hammond, 1643.

Themes

Why do events like hurricanes and floods occur? Why do disasters like the sinking of a ship happen? Why do some people die at an early age while others live a long and healthy life? Today we use science to answer these questions.

In 16th and 17th century Britain there were other answers. Many people explained how the world worked in terms of religion and magic. There was nothing strange in both going to church and believing in magic. Thus the death of a child was God's will; the sinking of a ship was the work of a witch. But not everybody explained events in these ways.

A small number of scientists were making new discoveries about the universe and people's place within it. They challenged older ways of thinking and tried to prove there were natural causes for events.

This chapter asks the following questions.

- How were witchcraft and magic used to explain events?

- How did older scientific ideas explain the world?

- How did new scientific ideas lead to what historians call the 'Scientific Revolution'?

The Focus looks at one way of explaining events - witchcraft. It is taken from a pamphlet, *News from Scotland*, an account of the Berwick Witch Trials published in 1591.

Focus Activities

1. How was the evidence from Gilly Duncan obtained? How reliable does this make it?

2. King James closely questioned Agnes Simpson. How might this have affected her answers?

3. Which was the most serious confession by Agnes? Explain why.

4. Do you find any of Agnes's confessions believable? Explain your answer.

5. Make a list of superstitions still found today. How many do you believe in? Why do some people still believe in them?

This evil witch

Charge	Witchcraft
Date	1590
Name	Agnes Simpson
Status	Elderly gentlewoman, living near Edinburgh
Accuser	Gilly Duncan, servant. She confessed to witchcraft and accused Agnes Simpson after torture by her master, David Seaton, deputy-bailiff of Tranent, Scotland.
Confession	After torture supervised by King James VI himself (later James I of England) Agnes Simpson confessed to the following evils.

King James questions Agnes Simpson – an illustration from *News from Scotland*, 1591.

Praying to the Devil.

Keeping a familiar (a magical spirit) in the form of a dog. This lived at the bottom of a well.

Attending a coven (gathering) of 90 witches and 6 warlocks (male witches) on All Hallows Eve. This cursed group sailed in riddles or sieves to North Berwick and danced a jig with Gilly Duncan.

Raising a great storm by fastening dead men's limbs on to the paws of a cat and throwing it into the sea.

Plotting to kill the King by:-

1. Hanging a black toad for 3 days to collect the poison. Soaking something belonging to His Majesty in the poison. This would make the King feel as if he had been lying upon sharp thorns and the ends of needles.

2. Attempting to cause a storm and wreck the King's ship on the way to Denmark.

Verdict   Death by strangulation and burning.

Witchcraft

Throughout history death, disease, storms, floods, droughts and famines have shown how little control people had over nature.

In 16th century Britain, believing in magic was a way of coping with and understanding such misfortunes. Unable to explain or control events by scientific means, people often relied on magic – on ghosts, goblins, spirits, charms, potions and wise men and women who could bring good or bad luck.

Many people lived in terror of witches. Witches had magical powers to cause injury and death. They might cause your crops to rot in the fields, your cattle and sheep to die from disease, your house to catch fire, your ship to sink, your family and friends to suffer from raging fevers, madness and death. The best way to protect yourself from witches was to find them and kill them.

In Britain a number of laws made the use of magic for evil a crime. Between 1542 and 1682 over 1000 witches were executed in England and Wales. Over 90% of those accused of witchcraft were women, usually the old and helpless. In most cases they were accused by neighbours who had suffered misfortunes such as an illness or the death of a child.

Source A

Villagers would travel miles to seek the advice of a cunning man (wizard) at a time when going two or three miles over bad roads was a good excuse not to go to church every week.

Keith Wrightson 'English Society, 1580-1680', 1982

Source B

I think I have heard of that man Jesus Christ once, in a play called a Corpus Christi play (a play about the Last Supper), where there was a man on a tree and the blood ran down.

An old man in 1640

Source D

That if any person:

(a) exercise any invocation (calling up) of any wicked spirit or shall consult, bargain with, entertain, feed or reward any wicked spirit or

(b) use any witchcraft, enchantment or sorcery causing someone to be killed, destroyed, wasted, consumed or lamed; then every such offender shall suffer pains of death.

New laws against witchcraft, 1604

Source C   The Witch Finder General

Matthew Hopkins called himself the Witch Finder General. In 1647 his book *The Discovery of Witches* was published. In it he describes 'his way of finding out witches'. The picture shows Elizabeth Clarke and her imps – demons who obeyed her. Hopkins had kept her awake for four nights waiting for her imps to appear. He describes one of them as follows.

'Vinegar Tom was like a long legged greyhound, with a head like an ox, with a long tail and broad eyes, who when his discoverer spoke to him immediately changed into the shape of a child of four years old without a head, gave half a dozen turns about the house and vanished at the door.'

Source E

Women being the weaker sex are more easily trapped by the devil's illusions. In all ages the devil hath won more with women than with men.

William Perkins, 'Discourse on the Damnable Art of Witchcraft', 1608

Source F   The Discovery of Witchcraft

The tales of witchcraft have taken deep root in the heart of man. For if any adultery, grief, sickness, loss of children, relatives or cattle happen to them, by and by they blame witches.

What treacherous and faithless dealing, what foolishness, what corruption and spitefulness, what cruelty, what abominable torture is practiced against these old women.

Reginald Scott, 'The Discovery of Witchcraft', 1584

Source G

A poster for the 1968 film, *Witchfinder General*, loosely based on the story of Matthew Hopkins.

Source H   Execution of witches, 1655

A. Hangman   B. Bellman   C. Two Sergeants
D. Witchfinder taking his money

Activities

1. Study Sources A and B. What do they tell you about the importance of religion in the lives of these people?

2. Look at Source C. Give your reasons for your answers to the following questions.

   a) Do you think Matthew Hopkins saw the imps?

   b) Do you think Elizabeth Clarke told him about the imps?

   c) Is this source useful to historians?

3. According to Source D what evil powers were witches feared to have? How does this source show that witches were taken as a serious threat?

4. a) According to Source E why were women usually blamed for witchcraft?

   b) Many of the women accused of witchcraft were old, helpless and lived alone. Why do you think these people were singled out?

5. What does Reginald Scott in Source F, think about the actions and ideas of men like Hopkins and Perkins? (Sources C and E)

6. Look at Source H.

   a) Explain what is happening in the picture.

   b) Why was the punishment for witchcraft death?

7. Why are witchcraft and the supernatural popular topics for films? (Source G)

Old science and new technology

At the beginning of the 16th century European scholars believed they could explain the workings of the human body, nature and the universe. Their explanations were based on ideas from the ancient Greeks, the beliefs of the Catholic Church and magic. These ideas formed the framework used by educated people to understand the world.

Yet at the same time there was a revival of learning, beginning in Italy. Historians call this the Renaissance – the word means rebirth. Scholars learned from and tried to improve on the discoveries and inventions of Greek and Roman civilisation.

Part of this was the result of new technology. New skills, for example in metal working, and inventions, such as the printing press, encouraged people to look at the world in a fresh light.

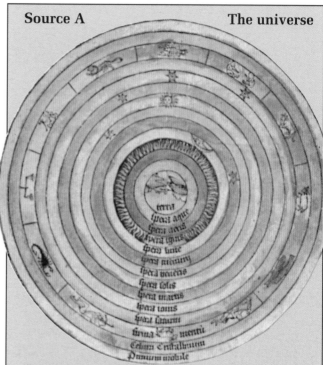

Source A   **The universe**

The universe based on the observations of the night sky by the ancient Greek, Ptolemy (AD 139-161). This view of the universe was also shared by the Christian Churches. Since God created the Earth on the 3rd day and the Sun, moon and stars on the 4th day, then the Earth must be the centre of the universe.

Source B   Elements

The Greek thinker Aristotle (384-322BC) explained that everything on earth was made from four elements. His followers would do this experiment to prove his ideas were correct.

Put a log in a fire: you will see **water** ooze out of the end; smoke will issue which is a sort of **air**; flames will appear which are **fire**: and ashes will be left, which are **earth**. So there are earth, air, fire and water in a log.

Source C   Alchemy

Gold was believed to be a metal with all four elements in perfect balance. Alchemy was the search for a way to control the elements and make gold. In February 1565, Cornelius de Lannoy, an alchemist promised Queen Elizabeth I that he would make her 50,000 marks of pure gold a year. When his experiments failed he was sent to the Tower of London. This engraving by Pieter Breughal the Elder shows alchemists at work.

Source D A Zodiac Man

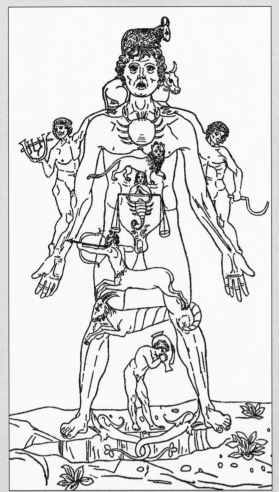

A Zodiac Man, a medical chart used by doctors in the Middle Ages to help them decide how to treat a patient. The instructions told the doctor at which times of the year it was unlucky to operate on various parts of the body. This was based on astrology, the study of the way in which the planets and stars were seen to affect people and nature.

Source E The printing press

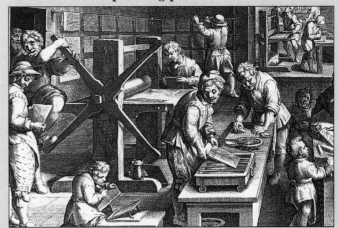

By 1500 printing presses were in use in every European country. Within 50 years more books had been printed than had been handwritten in the previous 1000 years.

Source F The cannon

By 1500 the cannon was the most fiercesome machine invented. As knowledge of metals developed, cannons became more powerful and less likely to explode when fired.

Activities

1. Ptolemy's view of the universe fitted closely with Christian beliefs. Explain how.

2. Using Source B can you think of any other apparently commonsense experiments that seem to prove the theory of the four elements? Think about things like snow or breath.

3. Take a careful look at Source C. What is Breughal's opinion of alchemists? How does he show this?

4. According to Source D what parts of your body should not be operated on on your birthday?

5. Think carefully about Sources E and F. They were the cutting edge of new technology around 1500. Can you suggest how they might encourage people to ask new questions about the world? What modern inventions might have the same effect today?

The Scientific Revolution, 1500-1700

Helped by the ideas of the Renaissance and new technology scientists began to question the view of the world inherited from the past. They challenged ideas that had been held for generations. To do this they developed a fresh approach that we take for granted today – careful observation backed by systematic experiments. In doing so they laid the foundations for modern science. So important was this change that historians have called it the 'Scientific Revolution'.

Source A

Sciences are vain and full of errors which are not born from experiment.

Leonardo da Vinci (1452-1519)

Source B

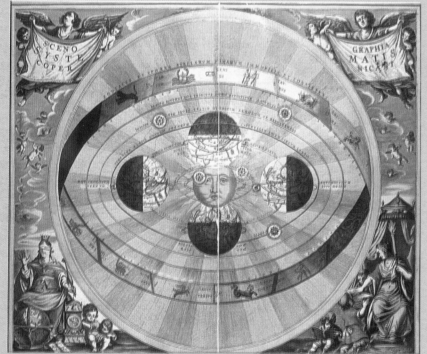

The universe based on the ideas and observations of Nicholas Copernicus (1473-1543). He argued that the Sun, not the Earth, was the centre of the universe and the planets orbited the Sun.

Source C

This man (Copernicus) wishes to turn astronomy upside down. But I believe in the Bible, since Joshua ordered the sun to stop turning round the earth for one day.

Martin Luther, 1540

Source D

Most scientists did not believe their ideas attacked belief in God. Isaac Newton wrote, 'This most beautiful system of sun, planets and comets could only proceed from the thinking and domination of an intelligent and powerful Being'.

Source E   Key figures of the Scientific Revolution

John Napier (1550-1617) worked out logarithms in 1614, giving scientists a precise system of calculation.

Galileo Galilei (1564-1642) used a telescope to sketch the moon and discover the moons of Jupiter.

William Harvey (1578-1657) proved that blood circulated around the body.

Robert Boyle (1627-1691) conducted key experiments on the part played by air in breathing and burning.

Robert Hook (1635-1703) was the first Curator (keeper) of Experiments for the Royal Society. He redesigned a telescope as a microscope.

Isaac Newton (1642-1727) developed the theory of gravity. The forces keeping the planets in orbit around the sun were the same as those that made an apple drop to earth.

Source F The Royal Society

The Royal Society was set up in England in 1662 to encourage scientific investigations.

Since their first founding they hath made a vast number of Experiments in almost all the works of nature. They have made particular enquiries into very many things of the Heavens, as well as of the Earth, Eclipses, Earthquakes, Fiery Eruptions, Floods, Mountains, Damps, Underground Fires, of Tides, Currents and Depths of the Sea, and many hundred other things.

E. Chamberlayne, 'The Present State of England', 1687

Source H

The Scientific Revolution is now usually seen as a turning point in world history. It was an extraordinary leap which had an effect on every aspect of thinking and life.

Hugh Kearney, 'Science and Change 1500-1700', 1971

Source G William Harvey

I have heard him say, that after his book of the Circulation of the Blood came out, that it was believed by the vulgar that he was crack brained. All the physicians were against his opinion. With much ado at last, in about 20 or 30 years time, it was accepted in all the universities in the world. He is the only man, perhaps, that ever lived to see his own ideas established in his lifetime.

John Aubrey, 1628

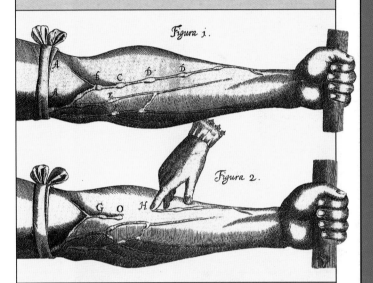

An illustration from William Harvey's book to show that valves in the veins only allowed blood to flow one way around the body.

Activities

1. Look at Source A and think about your science lessons. Why are experiments so important to scientists?

2. Compare the ideas of Copernicus in Source B with those of Ptolemy on page 72. What has changed? Why might this upset some Christians.

3. Why does Martin Luther (Source C) think Copernicus is wrong?

4. If Newton still believed in God would this make him a poor scientist? Explain your answer.

5. Match the modern sciences listed below with the names in Source E – Astronomy, Physics, Biology, Mathematics, Chemistry.

6. According to Source F how did the Royal Society encourage good science?

7. What effect did Harvey's discoveries have on his career? (Source G)

8. Bearing all the sources in mind suggest why Source H calls the Scientific Revolution 'an extraordinary leap' in history.

Checklist

- Between 1500 and 1750 most people believed in magic. This led to persecution of witches in the 17th century.

- Most educated people understood the world through a mixture of magic, religion and ideas from ancient Greece and Rome.

- The Scientific Revolution offered a new way of looking at the world and explanations of how nature worked.

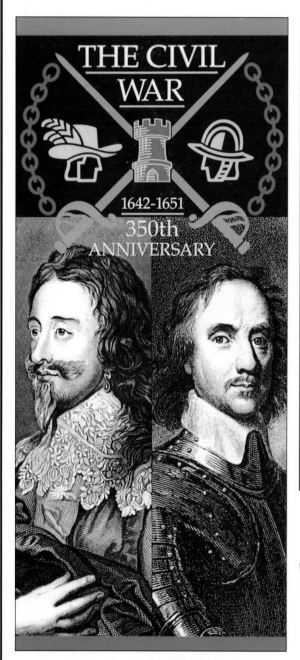

British history is an important part of the tourist industry. But how often do tourists understand that the quaint things they have been looking at may be evidence of troubled times in the past?

Themes

Most tourists visiting Britain today come because of the country's rich history. Their holiday might include a trip to see St Paul's Cathedral in London or paintings in the National Gallery.

If they stayed a little longer they might watch a Shakespeare play in Stratford or visit one of the great Elizabethan houses such as Longleat in Wiltshire. All of these things are part of British culture handed down from Tudor and Stuart times.

Historians, however, look at culture in a different way from tourists. A building or a play may carry hidden messages about how people lived and thought in the past. One such message is the way culture can be affected by politics and religion. For instance, the painting on the opposite page is not just a great work of art. The artist was hired to influence the way people thought about the king.

This chapter looks at examples of Tudor and Stuart culture and the way they were used to attack or defend ideas and governments.

The Focus looks at the way King Charles I used one of Europe's most famous painters to improve his image.

Focus Activities

Look carefully at the Focus painting and text. How does the artist set out to flatter the subject? Think! What is the king doing? How is he dressed? What is he riding through?

If this painting came up for auction today it would attract multi-million pound bids from around the world. If you were writing the auction catalogue describing it to possible buyers, what would you say? The following words have been used to describe Van Dyke's work. Use some of them to help you.

RHYTHM, MOVEMENT, THEATRICAL, DELICATE, SOPHISTICATED, REFINED, LUSTROUS, ENNOBLING, ROMANTIC, BOLD, SHIMMERING.

A painting fit for a king

A portrait of Charles I by Sir Anthony van Dyke

Since the Middle Ages Britain had been a backwater as far as painting was concerned. This began to change under the Stuart kings. James I wanted to show that his taste in the arts was as good as that of any other European monarch. He particularly wanted to prove his good taste to the important French and Spanish royal families.

For his son, Charles I, love of the arts was an essential part of being a king. He particularly liked paintings. In

1632 Charles was delighted when he persuaded the Dutch painter van Dyke to move to London. He was given a knighthood, the use of a house in Blackfriars and a grant of £200 a year. The king and the painter became good friends.

Van Dyke had been trained in the studios of the Flemish master Rubens and had worked for many years in Italy, the centre of the Renaissance. The work he was to do for Charles was as good as anything in Europe.

Printing and literacy

At the end of the Middle Ages reading and writing played little part in the lives of most people. By 1760 more than half the population was literate, that is could read and write.

The growing number of printing presses meant that books, newspapers, pamphlets and posters became more plentiful and much cheaper. Because of this, some historians have called the years after 1500 an 'information revolution'.

More information and greater literacy helped industry and business to develop. They also meant that people could learn more about what was happening in the country. By 1600, the people of Britain were amongst the best informed in Europe.

Governments realised that printing was one of the most important ways of spreading knowledge and ideas. They wanted to control it. The Crown claimed the right to regulate the publishing of all printed works. A printer who didn't have a licence could be put in prison.

Source B   Literacy

Date	Men	Women
1550	20%	5%
1650	30%	10%
1715	45%	25%
1760	60%	40%

This table gives an estimate of the people who could read and write.

Source D

Every man strains his fortune to keep his children at school. The cobbler will clout (hammer) till midnight, the porter will carry burdens till his bones crack, to give his son learning.

James Howell, 1651

Source A   The Great Bible

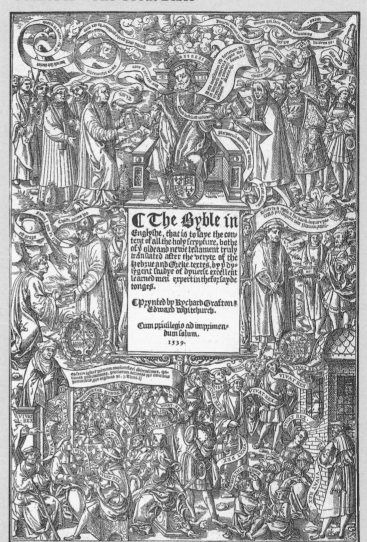

The best selling book was the Bible. This picture shows the cover of the Great Bible published in 1539 with the permission of Henry VIII. It was one of the first in English instead of Latin. The cover shows Henry in the image of God as the Supreme Head of the Church.

Source C

Soon the King took fright over this new English Bible. In 1543 he ordered Parliament to pass an Act forbidding, 'women, apprentices, journeymen (skilled workers), servingmen and labourers' to read it for themselves. This was because, 'that precious jewel, the Word of God, is argued over, rhymed, sung and jangled in every alehouse'.

Rosemary Kelly, 'A World of Change', 1987

Source E

A royalist cartoon showing Cromwell (B) working with the Devil

Source F

It was not easy for governments to control illegal newspapers. It was not easy to round up the peddlers who sold the papers on the streets. Editors used hand presses which might be crude but were also easy to carry. It needed but a few moments to pack up and load a press on to a handcart. London's honeycomb of closely packed streets provided lots of hiding places for secret presses that could be moved every few days.

Keith Williams, 'The English Newspaper', 1977

Source G

The Reformation is almost unthinkable without the invention of the printing press. From about 1560 England was flooded with books on reformed religion.

J.A. Sharpe, 'Early Modern England 1550-1760', 1986

Source H

Numb. 75.

A testimoniall of the valiant acts of the Plimouth Regiment. The King moves not towards Oxford. Four Northern Counties entring into Association. Crowland Abby said to be lost. Two Popes of Rome chosen. The Archbishop of Canterbury to come to his last Triall. Propositions of Peace almost finished. Colonell Wate, and Colonell Urrey two revolters, are come in againe to the Parliament with shame.

THE
KINGDOMES
Weekly Intelligencer:

SENT ABROAD
To prevent mis-information.

From *Tuesday* the 1. of *October*, to *Tuesday* the 8. of *October*, 1644.

This week hath produced little matter of Action in our Armies, I shall therefore in the first place informe you, of something done for the Armies, & concerning them. 1. The Parliament have voted (since my last) a Committee to go down to the Army, whose advice is to be taken by the Commander, or Commanders in chiefe ; I think the like course is taken in *Holland* : There are some of the States of the United Provinces, that do accompany the P. of *Orenge*, whose concurrent advice he takes upon any designe, & he takes this for no deminution of his command ; and how needfull this is in our Armies, the Kingdom is sensible of, considering what ill instruments have lately bin in the Army in the West, Ggg g which

This weekly newspaper supported the Parliamentary side in the Civil War.

Activities

1. Historians try to measure the number of people who could read and write in the past. One of the main ways is to count those who could sign their own names in the registers of births and marriages kept by local churches. Can you think of any problems with this method?

2. What do Sources B and D suggest about the education of women?

3. How does Source A show that Henry VIII wanted to control religion in his own country?

4. Read Source C. Why do you think Henry was worried about ordinary people reading the Bible?

5. List any other ways you can think of to spread new ideas without writing them down for others to read? With this in mind do you think Source G is likely to be an accurate comment?

6. During the Civil War both sides encouraged publicity for their cause. In what ways are Sources E and H trying to influence people.

7. Look at Source F. Can you suggest other ways a printer might avoid being caught?

Drama

Watching drama was one of the most popular entertainments. Rich and poor alike would flock to see a travelling group of players in the open air. In 1576 the first two purpose-built playhouses were opened in London.

As well as letting people enjoy themselves, drama was a powerful way of spreading ideas, especially amongst those who couldn't read. Again the government wanted control, as it did with the printed word. All new plays had to be approved by the Lord Chancellor.

Stuart Kings used drama to support their policies. This infuriated many Puritans who already disliked actors and plays. It even affected the career of William Shakespeare (1564-1616) the greatest playwright of the time. His main works were written in London for a company called the Chamberlain's Men. They were lucky to have the patronage, or protection, of the Court. At times this was needed to stop them being closed down by the Puritan council that ran London.

Source A

The Globe – one of London's main theatres. At the end of the 16th century there were weekly audiences of about 15,000 at London theatres. By 1605 as many as 2 out of 15 of the capital's population were going to the theatre every week.

Source B   James I

Know ye that We have licensed these our servants, Lawrence Fletcher, William Shakespeare, Richard Burbage freely to use and exercise the art and talent of playing for the recreation of our loving subjects, as well as for Our comfort and pleasure when we shall think good to see them.

James I licenced the Chamberlain's Men as his own theatre company in 1603. After this they became known as the King's Men.

Source C

This royal throne of Kings, this scepter'd isle,
This earth of majesty, this seat of Mars,
This other Eden, this demi-paradise,
This fortress built by nature for herself
Against infection, and the hand of war,
This happy breed of men, this little world,
This precious stone set in a silver sea,
Which serves it in the office of a wall,
Or as a moat defensive to a house,
Against the envy of less happier lands,
This blessed plot, this earth, this realm, this England.

An extract from Shakespeare's play 'Richard II'

Source D

Popular stage plays (the very pomp of the Devil) are sinful, heathen, rude, ungodly shows, and most wicked corruptions. They have been condemned in all ages as mischiefs to churches, to governments, to the manners, minds and souls of men.

The Puritan writer William Prynne in his book 'Histrio-Mastix, The Players Scourge', 1635

Source E

Guests at Sir Henry Unton's wedding feast were entertained by a masque. A masque usually told a story with singing, acting, music and dancing. This was a fashion from Italy and France taken up by the nobility.

Source F

It was the masque above all which served as a way to proclaim royal policies. Sometimes it was even the king who dictated the plot. Charles I wished to use the masque to educate his subjects in their duty to the sovereign.

Judith Hook, 'The Baroque Age in England', 1976

Source G

England, threatened with a Cloud of Blood, by a Civil War, needs all possible means to avoid the Wrath of God. It is therefore thought fit by Parliament that while these sad causes continue the public stage plays shall cease.

A law passed by a Puritan Parliament in 1642

Activities

1. In 1605 London had a population of about 200,000. Using Source A work out how many people went to the theatre at least once a week?

2. Look at Sources B and C. Who, and in what way, is Shakespeare trying to please. Why might he be doing this?

3. The rich used masques to show off their wealth. Look at Source E. What evidence is there to show that Sir Henry had spent a lot of money?

4. Using Sources D and G list the reasons why many Puritans disliked drama and eventually banned it.

5. Using Sources B, C and F, can you suggest other reasons why Puritans might feel hostile to actors and plays?

Architecture

Buildings, like paintings, printing or drama, are sometimes used for political or religious purposes. The design, the site, the money and the materials used to build them can all be influenced by the events of the time.

The Reformation brought an end to the dynamic church and cathedral building that had gone on throughout the Middle Ages. In the years after 1530 many churches were altered or damaged by Protestants offended by what they saw as symbols of Catholicism – statues, wall paintings, stained glass windows and altar rails. New churches were built to meet the needs of Protestant ways of worship.

By the 16th century most of Britain was a safer place to live. Towns began to grow beyond the protection of their medieval walls. The nobility increasingly gave up their cold castles for great country houses. These became the new symbols of their wealth and power. Yet in the Civil War old castles and town walls proved remarkably good at holding off modern armies.

Source A   St Stephen's Church

Sir Christopher Wren was the architect for St Stephen's, Walbrook, in London. Wren designed 53 churches to replace those burnt down in the Great Fire of London in 1666. St Stephen's, is one of his best. It was built to fit Protestant ideas about churches – plainer, more open, with more light. The congregation could see the vicar throughout the service and listen to a rousing sermon.

Source B   Warmington Church

Warmington Church, Northants is a typical parish church built in the Middle Ages. The altar was at the end of the chancel, usually hidden from the congregation by a highly decorated screen. Only the priest could go into this area.

Source C Longleat

Longleat in Wiltshire, one of the earliest great Elizabethan houses. It was built in the 1560s and painted here by the Flemish artist Jan Siberechts in 1675.

Source D

What the aristocrats demanded of their architects was that they should build them country houses on their estates which have all the appearances of palaces. They were thought of as works of art rather than homes.

Judith Hook, 'The Baroque Age in England', 1976

Source E Corfe Castle

Corfe Castle was defended several times by Lady Bankes against Parliamentary armies. After the Civil War it was 'slighted' on the orders of Parliament. This means crucial parts of the defences were destroyed. This happened to castles and manor houses across the country.

Activities

1. Compare Sources A and B. How and why are they different?
2. Country houses were designed to show off the importance of their owners. How might a modern estate agent describe Source C?
3. Using Source C, would you agree or disagree with Source D? Explain why.
4. Castles were old fashioned by 1640. How did the Civil War suddenly make them important again? (Source E)

Checklist

- Printing led to more information being available to ordinary people than ever before. This helped to spread new ideas.
- The Stuart kings used drama to support their rule. After the Civil War Parliament closed the theatres.
- The way buildings are used or designed can be evidence of important political, religious or social changes.

A bigger kind of ship, called a carrack, was built in the 16th century. It was designed to sail across oceans, unlike earlier top-heavy ships that had to keep close to coastlines.

Ternate, one of the Spice Islands. It was the main source for cloves.

A 12th century map of the world

Themes

From the late 1400s onwards European seamen made use of improvements in shipbuilding and navigation to find new routes to the Spice Islands east of India. Their voyages through uncharted seas to lands previously unknown to them changed the way Europeans understood the world.

They discovered that the world was much bigger than they had imagined, that all the oceans were connected, that a continent lay to the west of Europe, which they called America. Europeans were attracted to make risky explorations in the hope of making fortunes through trade.

This chapter looks at the following questions.

- How did Britain develop into the most powerful trading nation in the world?

- What were the attitudes of Europeans to colonised peoples?

We begin this chapter as a Tudor schoolboy Richard Hakluyt (pronounced 'hak-loot') visits his older cousin in 1568.

Focus Activities

1. What are the main differences between:
   a) the map of the world in the twelfth century,
   b) Mercator's map, c) a map of the world today?

2. a) Explorers returned with stories of strange people in far-off lands. Imagine one of these stories and describe a strange person. Your neighbour now has to draw the person using your spoken description.

   b) Why did some people believe that creatures like those in the picture on the opposite page actually existed?

A world of wonder

Richard Hakluyt loved to visit his cousin. He looked all around the room. Lying open on a table were books with strange pictures of distant lands and curious animals. Best of all were the maps of the world; a world of wonder far beyond his small circle of friends and family.

People feared that monsters lived in unknown lands.

Seeing the boy's interest, Richard's cousin began to speak of the riches in these lands, of their special fruits and animals and fishes, and most of all of the possibility of finding gold and silver there. Richard's eyes widened in astonishment and his imagination filled with pictures. Of ships with billowing sails cutting through dark green oceans; sighting thin strips of strange coastlines set in empty blue skies. Of wharves crowded with watermen and sailors; carts carrying goods grinding over cobblestones; the squeal of block and tackle as timbers, fish and fruit swung from ship to quayside.

He never forgot that visit and long afterwards said the experience sank deep into his memory. Although he travelled no further than France, Hakluyt devoted his life to collecting and writing down information about the explorations of his time. In 1589 his book called *The Principal Navigations of the English Nation* was published. It describes the first few steps taken by the Elizabethan sailors on the path to Britain's trading empire.

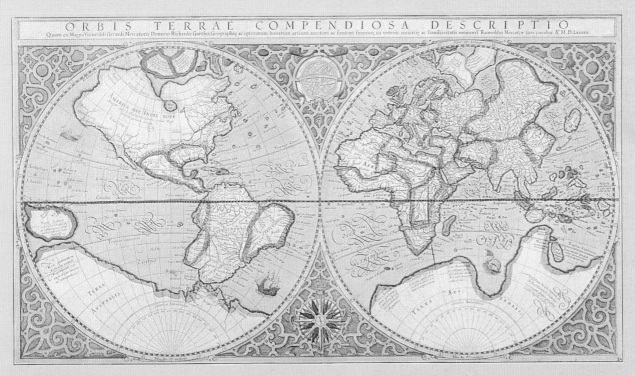

One of the most important maps showing the new discoveries was drawn by Mercator in 1538.

Beginnings of Empire

Richard Hakluyt published his book with the aim of praising, 'the works of the Lord and his wonders in the deep'. It was also in praise of the bravery of English explorers. Hakluyt was convinced that the explorations were of benefit not just to Europeans but also to non-Europeans. Not only would everyone's lives improve with better food and clothes, but non-Europeans could also learn and copy the 'civilised' ways of Europeans.

Source A

A fight between English explorers and Eskimos. This was drawn by John White, who sailed with Martin Frobisher in an attempt to find a route around the north of Canada in 1577.

Source B   English explorers

Englishmen have always been searchers of remote parts of the world and so during the most famous government of her most excellent majesty they have excelled all the nations and people of this earth.

They return from all corners of the world, richly laden with goods. We must take as our example the Kings of Spain and Portugal, who have not only enlarged their empires, greatly enriched themselves and their subjects, but have also trebled the numbers of their ships and sailors. It is certain that the strength of our country depends on the number of ships and sailors we possess. Many of these ships have been for the fishing trade only. If our countrymen were once planted in North America they might not only fish all year round but also increase our fleet.

It is well known that all savages, as soon as they begin to taste civilisation will take to it, be it ever so simple. They will make great efforts for a simple shirt and cap. This will give great opportunities to sell our English clothes and give work to many. And those that lie idle in our country can be put to work making trifling things.

These voyages, however, are not undertaken just for ourselves and our country. The savages will bless the hour when they hear of the gladsome tidings of Jesus Christ, by which means they can be brought from living lies to knowing the truth. They will learn how to make their land grow more, but above all they will learn to have civilised government.

Richard Hakluyt, 'The Principal Navigations of the English Nation', 1589

Source C   Trade and empire, 1750

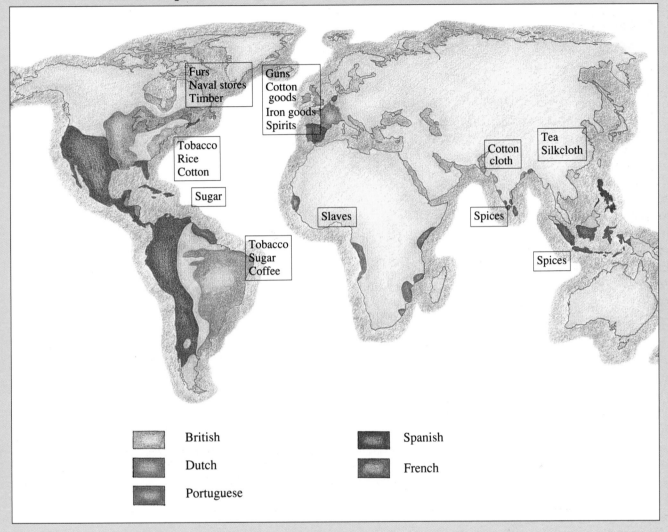

Furs
Naval stores
Timber

Guns
Cotton goods
Iron goods
Spirits

Tobacco
Rice
Cotton

Sugar

Cotton cloth

Tea
Silkcloth

Tobacco
Sugar
Coffee

Slaves

Spices

Spices

British   Spanish

Dutch   French

Portuguese

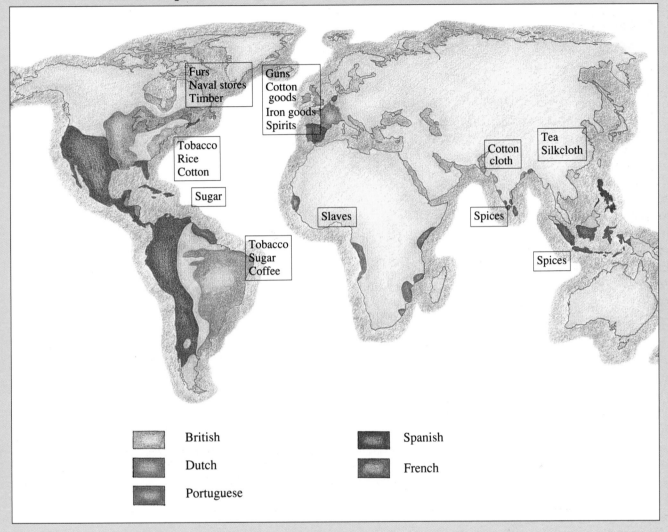

Activities

1. Look at Source A. Why might disputes like this occur?

2. Read Source B.

   a) According to Richard Hakluyt why should Englishmen explore and trade with other parts of the world?

   b) In what ways does Richard Hakluyt show that he feels Englishmen in particular and Europeans in general, are superior to other people?

3. Look at Source C.

   a) Which of Richard Hakluyt's hopes has come to pass? (Source B)

   b) What were the advantages of opening up sea routes rather than overland routes?

   c) What benefits would there be for those countries that grew strong in trade?

   d) Why might trading with other parts of the world lead to attempts to colonise them by Europeans?

The slave trade

Richard Hakluyt's belief that all things European were superior was an attitude shared by most of his fellow Europeans. At best this meant that people of other continents were to be treated as children and taught to behave like Europeans. At worst it meant treating them as possessions to be bought and sold in the market place.

It was this last view that led to the development of the slave trade. First, convicts were shipped over from Europe to cultivate cotton and tobacco plantations in America. But they were not used to the climate and died off quickly. Besides, there were never enough of them.

The answer was found when an enterprising merchant landed in West Africa in 1518, bought some prisoners from an African chief, shipped them across the Atlantic and sold them to the plantation owners as slaves. Fortunes were to be made from this human cargo and much of England's wealth grew from the slave trade. Over 9 million slaves were imported into the Americas during the next 350 years, nearly 2 million into British colonies. It was not until 1833, through the efforts of William Wilberforce and the Anti-Slavery Society, that slavery was finally abolished throughout the British Empire.

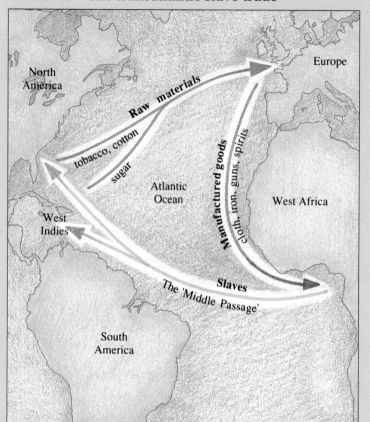

Source A   The transatlantic slave trade

The 'triangular trade'. Ships sailed from England with manufactured goods which were exchanged for slaves in Africa. The slaves were taken across the Atlantic and sold in the West Indies, North and South America. The ships returned loaded with the products of the plantations.

Source B

This is a model of a slave ship which William Wilberforce had made for the House of Commons to show the cruel conditions aboard. Each slave had a space of about five feet by two. A fifth to one-third of them were expected to die during the voyage. Even then, huge profits could be made.

Source C

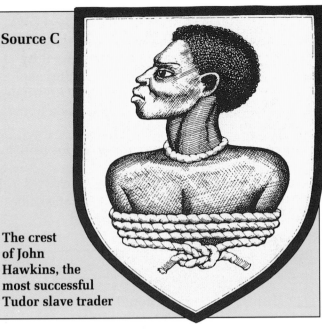

The crest of John Hawkins, the most successful Tudor slave trader

Source D

I've purchased nine negro slaves and I was shocked at the first appearance of human flesh set up for sale. But surely God created them for the use and benefit of us, otherwise he would have given us a sign to say different.

John Finney, a sugar plantation owner, 1726

Source E

TO BE SOLD, on board the Ship *Bance-Island*, on tuesday the 6th of *May* next, at *Ashley-Ferry*; a choice cargo of about 250 fine healthy NEGROES, just arrived from the Windward & Rice Coast. —The utmost care has already been taken, and shall be continued, to keep them free from the least danger of being infected with the SMALL-POX, no boat having been on board, and all other communication with people from *Charles-Town* prevented.

Austin, Laurens, & Appleby.

Source F   Slavery in Britain – legal rulings

1569   It was decided that England has 'too pure an air for slaves to breathe'.

1701   As soon as a negro comes to England, he becomes free.

1706   By the common law no man can have property in another.

Source G   Black people against slavery

There were many who raised their voices against slavery. Ottobah Cugoano was a slave who was born in 1757. Escaping to England he later published a short book setting out the case for the abolition of slavery.

'I saw a slave receive twenty-four lashes of the whip for being seen in church instead of going to work. Britain should be the first to abolish this evil trade for she has acquired a greater share in the trade than all the rest together. They are the first that ought to set an example.'

Ottobah Cugoano, 'Thoughts and Sentiments on the Evil and Wicked Traffic of the Human Species', 1787

Activities

1. Study Source A.

   a) Why would the transatlantic slave trade be so profitable to ship owners?

   b) Why was it called the 'triangular trade'?

2. Study Sources B, C, D and E. What do they show about European attitudes towards the slave trade?

3. Read Source F. Why might there be a difference in attitude to the keeping of slaves in Britain compared to the Americas?

4. Read Source G. Why does Ottobah Cugoano think that Britain should be the first to abolish the slave trade?

Trade, wealth and power

In the race for overseas trade Britain had to compete with Spain, France and Holland. The result was that Britain became involved in wars with all these countries. By the mid-18th century she had emerged the clear winner. With this achievement came the prize of empire. From a few struggling settlements scattered along the bleak north-eastern coast of America had grown thirteen booming colonies. Added to this were wealthy sugar producing islands in the West Indies and trading posts in Africa and India. By 1770 Britain had added large parts of India and Canada to her conquests.

The colonies provided raw materials for British industry as well as a market for British manufactured goods. In this way Britain's industrial strength began to grow until she came to be called the 'workshop of the world'.

Source A   Trading companies

The British government could not protect trade in so many distant parts of the world. Merchants formed themselves into trading companies and provided for their own defence with expensive forts and ships of war. Each company was given a charter by the government which meant only they could trade in that part of the world. For example, the East India Company was given a charter in 1601 for trade with India and the Spice Islands, the Hudson's Bay Company in 1670 for trade with Canada. This picture shows Robert Clive in 1765 receiving from the Mogul Emperor the right of the East India Company to control Bengal.

Source B   Imports and exports

In the 18th century Britain's main imports were sugar, cotton, silk, spices, tea, coffee and timber. Her main exports were wool, wheat, salt and manufactured goods. Ports such as Bristol, Liverpool, Whitehaven and London grew rapidly. The fastest growth was in the western ports of Bristol and Liverpool due mainly to the rise in trade with North America and the West Indies. This picture shows the Broad Quay at Bristol in 1735.

Source C

Our trade has been greatly increased. At the beginning of the century our exports to the colonies were only one twelfth of our total exports. They are now more than one third of the whole. This is the importance of the colonies to us.

Edmund Burke MP in a speech to the House of Commons, 1775

Source D

A battle between the British and Dutch fleets, 1673

Source E

Britain fought a number of wars with her trading rivals – with Holland (1552-54, 1665-67, 1672-74), Spain (1653-59, 1740-48) and France (1690-1715, 1756-63). Often these wars involved competition for trade and colonies. The first war with Holland stemmed from disputes between the British and Dutch in North America, the West Indies, Africa, India and the East Indies.

Charles Wilson, 'England's Apprenticeship, 1603-1763', 1965

Source F

The British defeat the French at Quebec in Canada, 1759

Activities

With the help of your neighbour write a speech to your fellow merchants at a banquet in the Guild Hall in London. Refer to:

- the growth of trade since the days of Elizabeth,
- the benefits of empire to Britain,
- the defeat of Britain's enemies.

Checklist

- In 1500 Britain was a small trading nation. By 1750 Britain had the largest fleet and empire in the world.

- The empire provided raw materials for Britain's growing industry as well as a huge market for her manufactured goods.

Time does not stand still. A great deal of change has happened in your own lifetime. Suppose you were able to speak to your ancestors in 1750. What would you tell them about all the changes that have occurred since their time?

Now imagine what a conversation might have been like between your ancestors of 1500 and 1750. What would they recognise as similar to both their ages? What would have changed?

Let's take up five major themes which have run through the book:

- Crown and Parliament
- Changes in religion
- The making of the United Kingdom
- Britain's place in the world
- The development of science

Timespeak

1500

1750

What monarch rules your time by God's good grace?

His gracious majesty George II by aid of Parliament ...

You shock me! No monarch was the servant of a prattling Parliament in my day ...

At least I can imagine there can be no change with the Holy Mother Catholic Church ...

England is a Protestant country ...

Protestant! What heretic nonsense is that...?

No heretic nonsense but the true faith ...

Then if that be true, England must be a poor nation...

On the contrary the United Kingdom is the most powerful nation in the world ...

Saints preserve us ... we were a tiny island ...

Not the saints, but science and trade ...

Crown and Parliament

Source A The monarchy today

The monarch is still head of state. However, power has passed to Parliament, the Cabinet, the Prime Minister and the law courts. Royal assent (agreement) is still needed before bills become law. The monarch can still make treaties with other countries and even declare war. But in practice these decisions are made by the political party that forms the government. The monarch is 'advised' in all these matters by the Prime Minister and other government ministers. Today the queen is a symbolic head of state, a figurehead without real power.

David Roberts, 'Politics: A New Approach', 1986

Source B

Queen's speech at the state opening of Parliament. She announces the things which the political party in power intends to make into law.

Source C

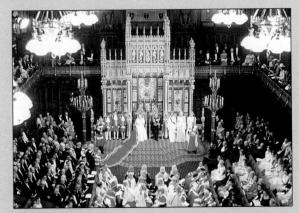

State opening of Parliament. Every year the monarch officially opens a new session of Parliament.

Source D

The House of Lords still has the power to discuss bills before they become law. However, they can no longer prevent a bill from becoming law, only delay it.

Activities

1. Look at the conversations on the facing page.

    a) Draw five sets of paired boxes like this

1500	1750

    to show the five themes. Draw symbols in each pair of boxes and write short captions to explain the main changes between 1500 and 1750.

    b) Read the conversations. Add a sentence to replace each set of dots (...).

2. Queen Elizabeth II is a symbolic head of state. Explain what this means using Sources A and B.

3. Why do you think the monarch still opens Parliament? (Sources B and C)

4. Some people want to abolish both the monarchy and the House of Lords (Source D). Do you think either should be abolished? Give reasons for your answer.

A United Kingdom?

Scotland, Wales and Northern Ireland all have political parties which seek to break away from the United Kingdom. So far none of these parties has won the majority of the votes in these countries. The Scottish National Party in Scotland and Plaid Cymru in Wales both want independence for their countries and membership of the European Community. In Northern Ireland, Sinn Fein wants a united Ireland, separate from the UK. In England, the Labour Party supports a united Ireland achieved by agreement and without violence. Labour and the Liberal Democrats both support devolution for Scotland and Wales. This means 'home rule' with a Scottish Parliament and a Welsh Assembly. The Conservative Party is against devolution and a united Ireland.

Source A   The 1992 Election

Scotland
72 seats

	Votes	Seats
Labour	39.0%	49
Conservative	25.7%	11
Scottish National Party	21.5%	3
Liberal Democrat	13.1%	9
Other	0.8%	0

Wales
38 seats

	Votes	Seats
Labour	49.5%	27
Conservative	28.6%	6
Liberal Democrat	12.4%	1
Plaid Cymru	8.8%	4
Other	0.7%	0

Northern Ireland
17 seats

	Votes	Seats
Ulster Unionist Party	30.7%	9
SDLP	15.0%	4
Alliance Party	12.4%	0
DUP	11.6%	3
Conservative	11.0%	0
Sinn Fein	10.0%	0
Other	9.4%	1

Source B

The devolution proposals put forward by the Liberal Democrats and Labour alike would put us on the road to a Disunited Kingdom. The UK is in danger. Wake up my fellow countrymen. Wake up now before it is too late.

John Major, Leader of the Conservative Party, during the election campaign, 1992

Source C

In 1922 Southern Ireland (now called Eire) became independent from the UK. Northern Ireland remains part of the UK but is bitterly divided between Catholics and Protestants. This recent photograph shows a statue of William of Orange on a Protestant house in Belfast.

All the main political parties see the UK's future as a member of the European Community. But some people fear that the United Kingdom will simply merge into a united Europe and eventually disappear as a separate country. Parliament will lose its power and the country its independence.

Others, however, do not see closer union with Europe as seriously reducing the power of Parliament or leading to the disappearance of the UK into a united Europe.

Activities

1. Judging from Source A, do the people of Scotland, Wales and Northern Ireland want independence from the UK?

2. Do you agree with John Major (Source B)? Give reasons for your answer.

3. a) Why do you think there is a statue of William of Orange on this house? (Source C)

   b) A knowledge of history is necessary to understand the situation in Northern Ireland today. Do you agree? Give reasons for your answer.

4. What do you think about the design of the UK's ECUs? Would you include the queen's head in the design?

5. Are you in favour of the United Kingdom's membership of the European Community? Explain your answer.

Source D

Whenever a major change in coinage seems likely, new pattern or prototype coins are created. This source shows a pattern ECU set for the UK. ECU stands for European Currency Unit which will become the currency of the European Community. Mints in France, Spain, Holland, Belgium, Eire and the UK have already produced pattern ECUs for their countries.

Acknowledgements

Cover   Caroline Waring-Collins (Waring Collins Partnership)

Illustrations   Caroline Waring-Collins (Waring Collins Partnership)

Computer generated artwork   Elaine Marie Cox (Waring Collins Partnership)

Page design   Andrew Allen

Picture credits

All Saints Church 67 (r); All Saints College, Oxford 62; Andrew Allen 5 (r), 95; Ancient Art and Architecture Collection 52; Ashmolean Museum 16, 24, 45; BFI Stills, Posters and Designs 71 (l); Blairs College Museum 27 (b); Bodleian Library 37 (r); Bridgeman Art Library 83 (t), 84 (t), 90 (b); British Library 9 (t), 90 (t); C.M. Dixon 26 (t), 94; Fotomas Index 14, 31, 57, 68, 86; Glasgow Museums and Art Galleries 23; Hulton Picture Company 33, 34, 37, 41, 73 (t); A.F Kersting 82 (tr); Laing Art Gallery, Newcastle upon Tyne (Tyne and Wear Museums) 49; Mansell Collection 36, 43 (r), 89; Mary Evans Picture Library 25, 60 (t), 67 (l), 69, 72 (b), 74, 85 (t), 85 (b); National Portrait Gallery 5 (l and m), 9 (m), 17, 18, 22, 30, 32, 40 (l and r), 46, 54, 81; Peter Newark's Historical Pictures 78, 80, 91 (b); Picturepoint 58 (bl), 60 (m and b), 65, 83 (b); Royal Collection, reproduced by gracious permission of Her Majesty the Queen 19, 55, 73 (br), 77; Scottish National Portrait Gallery 29; Sidney Sussex College, reproduced by permission of the Master and Fellows 42; Sir John Soane's Museum, 47; St Stephen's Church 82 (b); Topham Picture Source 36 (br and l), 93 (t and m); University of Cambridge Committee for Aerial Photography 13; Warmington Church 82 (m and bl); Wilberforce House Museum 88 (b); Woodmansterne 91 (t), 93 (b).

Every effort has been made to locate the copyright owners of material used in this book. Any omissions brought to our attention are regretted and will be credited in subsequent printings.

Causeway Press Ltd
PO Box 13, Ormskirk, Lancashire L39 5HP

© Peter Hepplewhite and Neil Tonge 1992

1st impression 1992

British Library Cataloguing in Publication Data - a catalogue record for this book is available from the British Library.

ISBN 0 946183 94 5

Typesetting by John A. Collins, Elaine Marie Cox (Waring Collins Partnership), Ormskirk, Lancashire L39 1QR

Printed and bound by Butler & Tanner Ltd, Frome and London